بسم الله الرحمن الرحيم

AL-ARBAʿĪN COLLECTION

# AL-ARBAʿĪN

## On His ﷺ Noble Character

IMAM YŪSUF AL-NABAHĀNĪ

*Translation & Notes by*

Ali Saiyed

firasah

TITLE: *Al-Arbaʿīn*: On His ﷺ Noble Character

Copyright: Firasah Publications
Website: www.firasah.org
ISBN: 978-1-73930-880-3

PUBLISHED BY: Firasah Publications
PUBLISHED IN: Shaʿbān 1444AH / March 2023



AUTHORED BY: Imam Yūsuf al-Nabahānī
TRANSLATION & NOTES BY: Ali Saiyed

DESIGN & TYPESETTING BY: TypeRyt (info@typeryt.com)

## *Dedication*

This book is dedicated to my mother thrice, my father, my sister, and my brothers, Ammaar and Muhammad Zahid.

# *Acknowledgments*

I would like to express my gratitude to everyone who has contributed to this work. I would like to extend special thanks to the following individuals:

- Shaykh Abu Hasan, whose invaluable guidance throughout the book, especially on analysing and understanding Hadith from the perspective of Prophetic love, has been truly inspiring.
- Mufti Kalim al-Misbahi who kindly agreed to read over the text through the lens of his.
- Brother Hassan, who has been a reliable source of thoughts, ideas, and suggestions throughout.
- Hafiz Ismail, whose feedback has consistently pushed me to enhance my work. Truly, good counsel is an essential part of the religion.
- Brothers Muhammad Patel, Hafiz Safwan Bashir, and Farhan Mashhadi, who have proofread the text and assisted me in putting this book together.

- My dear friends Yusuf Bux and Oveis Patel, who have always supported me in any religious endeavours I have pursued since I embarked on my journey as a student of knowledge.
- My brother Ammaar for his willingness to help me in whatever way he can.
- Sidi Mostafa Azzam, who kindly allowed me to use some of his poetry translations from al-Burda.
- My students, Muhammad Faizan and Muhammad Zahid, who devoted countless hours in proofreading, checking references, and preparing the bibliography. May Allah grant them beneficial knowledge and make them true scholars of the religion.
- Finally, there were many others who provided moral support and encouragement, as well as proofreading the text, although I cannot name them all, I will always keep them in my prayers. May Allah reward each and every one of you.

Whatever good is in the book is from Allah, who assisted me with the likes of the above individuals. Whilst, if there are any mistakes or errors then it is solely due to me.

*Author's Biography*[1]

# YŪSUF AL-NABAHĀNĪ

HE IS YŪSUF IBN ISMĀʿĪL IBN YŪSUF IBN ISMĀʿĪL ibn Muḥammad Nāṣir al-Dīn al-Nabahānī. Born in the village of Ijzim, Palestine, in 1265/1849, he read the Qur'an under the tutelage of his father, the righteous scholar and meticulous memoriser of the Qur'an, Shaykh Ismāʿīl al-Nabahānī. Part of his father's litany was to recite at least a third of the Qur'an daily, thereby completing its recital three times a week.

In 1283/1866, his father sent him to Egypt to study the sacred sciences. He pursued his studies at al-Azhar, where he remained until 1289/1872. During this period, he studied the core sciences of the Shariah and its ancillary disciplines under the tutelage of some of its most prominent and

---

1 Taken from Shaykh Amjad Mahmood's, *Muhammad ﷺ: A Qur'anic Exposition of His Excellence and Virtues*. Published by Heritage Press.

accomplished scholars. The most notable and senior of these was Shaykh Ibrāhīm al-Saqqā al-Shāfiʿī, who died in 1298 AH at approximately ninety years of age, having spent most of his life imparting sacred knowledge to students; most scholars of the time were either his direct or indirect students. The author attended his lessons for a period of three years, studying Shafi'i jurisprudence with him. His teachers also include:

- Shaykh al-Sayyid Muḥammad al-Damanhūrī (d. 1286).
- Shaykh Ibrāhīm al-Zurrū al-Khalīlī (d. 1287).
- Shaykh Aḥmad al-Ajhūrī al-Darīr (d. 1293),
- Shaykh Ḥasan al-ʿAdawī (d. 1298),
- Shaykh al-Sayyid ʿAbd al-Hādī Najā al-Abyārī (d. 1305).
- Shaykh Shams al-Dīn Muḥammad al-Anbābī al-Shāfiʿī (d. 1313),
- Shaykh ʿAbd al-Raḥmān al-Shirbīnī al-Shāfiʿī (d. 1326),
- ʿAbd al-Qādir al-Rāfiʿī al-Ḥanafī al-Ṭarabulsī (d.1323),
- Shaykh Yūsuf al-Barqāwī al-Ḥanbalī (d. 1320) among many others.

After graduation from al-Azhar, he returned to his hometown town of Ijzim, where he began to disseminate sacred knowledge, in addition to teaching in Akka. He travelled to Beirut and Damascus, where he met eminent scholars. In the latter he met the foremost jurist, the Mufti of *Shām* at the time, Sayyid Maḥmūd Effendī al-Ḥamzāwī. He had the privilege of reading the beginning of *Ṣaḥīḥ al-Bukhārī* with him, after which Sayyid Maḥmūd granted him a general license (*al-ʿijāzah al-ʿāmmah*) comprising the remainder of the canonical hadith collections, as well all his other narrations and works.

He later travelled twice to Constantinople and worked there for several years as an editor and proofreader for Arabic books, periodicals and literature. He was then appointed Head Judge of al-Jaza' court in the Syrian coastal city of Latakia in 1300/1883. Five years later the government assigned him to be Chief Judge of Jerusalem and then promoted him to the position of Chief Justice of Beirut in 1305/1888 where he served until his retirement. In the year 1310/1893, he performed the hajj and also stayed in Medina for a period.

After retirement, he dedicated himself to writing and religious devotion. He penned over fifty works in various Islamic disciplines, such as jurisprudence, theology, hadith, prophetic biography, heresiology and Sufism. The following are just a few of these:

- *Ḥujjat Allāh ʿalā al-ʿālamīn* (Allah's Proof against All Beings)
- *Saʿādat al-dārayn fī ṣalāh ʿalā sayyid al-kawnayn* ﷺ (Felicity in both Abodes through sending Blessings upon the Master of the Two Worlds)
- *Waṣā'il al-wuṣūl fī shamā'il al-rasūl* ﷺ (The Means of

Knowing the Characteristics of the Messenger)
- *Jāmiʿ karāmāt al-awliyāʾ* (Compendium of the Miracles of Saints)
- *Mukhtaṣar Riyāḍ al-Ṣāliḥīn* (Abridgement of the Gardens of the Righteous)

He would frequent Medina to visit the Prophet ﷺ and would spend the winters there. He passed away in Beirut in Ramadan 1350/1932.

# INTRODUCTION

In the name of Allah, The Most Compassionate, The Most Merciful.

All praise is for Allah, the Lord of the Worlds, the One who created all things in a perfect manner and guided humanity with the one who came as the Excellent Example. May peace and blessings descend upon the Prophet Muhammad, who was sent by Allah to perfect character, and upon his Progeny, Companions, and all those who follow in his footsteps striving for excellence.

The Prophet Muhammad ﷺ came with a profound and potent message that changed the course of human history in a manner that remains unparalleled. He transformed a decadent society into an exemplar of virtue and piety, one that came to be defined by its unwavering devotion to Allah and its commitment to Him. This message is simple yet all-encompassing: There is no god but Allah, and Muhammad is His Messenger.

Muslims around the world worship none but Allah, and yet it is only by following the embodied wisdom of His Prophets, and most notably the paragon of the Prophet Muhammad ﷺ that a person can attain felicity in this world and the next. The earliest generations of Muslims dedicated themselves to studying and emulating his every teaching, behaviour, and character. His example transcends outward actions and words, but rather also reflects the purity of his inner being: his unwavering heart, his closeness to Allah, and his uncompromising commitment to goodness, beauty and righteousness.

*He reached the pinnacle with his perfection*
*He illuminated the world with his beauty*
*How excellent are all of his characteristics*
*Salutations upon him and his progeny*

SHAYKH SAʿDĪ

Character, according to the ancient Greeks, is a symbol or imprint upon the soul. In Arabic, linguists describe '*Khuluq ʿaẓīm*' as an intuitive disposition that inclines a person towards good. In this sense, good character is an attribute of the soul, attained through the process of purification and training until seeking and enacting good becomes its second nature. In this age of moral murkiness, it is as important as it ever was that

Muslims strive to remodel their way of being, both in terms of their outer and their inner, in a way that is determined by the Muhammadan way.

Realigning one's behaviour in light of the Muhammadan character is not merely recommended but is rather an obligation upon every believer in Islam. The Prophets are not just the vehicles of Allah's guidance but beings who represent it to the utmost degree. Thus, the life and ethical character of the Prophet Muhammad ﷺ is of paramount importance, a subject so vast and profound, such that scholars have written entire volumes exploring its various facets from a multitude of perspectives. This concise work serves as an introduction to some of the Prophet's ﷺ most prominent characteristics, and serves as an inception point to learn more about him.

In writing this book, I have drawn upon traditional Islamic scholarship as well as the insights of prominent non-Muslim figures who recognised the greatness of the Prophet Muhammad's character ﷺ. The purpose of quoting non-Muslim personalities was to show that people, some who were even critical of Islam, could not but acknowledge the Prophet Muhammad's ﷺ awe-inspiring personality. Indeed, and how could they not? It was the Lord, Most High, who elevated him above all and made him the most perfect being in His creation.

I hope that those who read this book come to better appreciate the Prophet Muhammad's ﷺ timeless character and his way of being. May Allah allow me, first and foremost, to follow the example of the Prophet Muhammad ﷺ and learn from his teachings. I pray that this work will serve as a source of edification and spiritual upliftment to people across the world so it can serve as a means of reward for me and all those who assisted me in this work. May Allah accept this humble effort and make it solely for His sake.

ALI SAIYED

# THE HUE OF MORAL EXCELLENCE

Al-Ḥabīb ʿUmar bin Ḥafīẓ

All praise be to Allah, the Sovereign, the Creator. And may Allah send peace and salutations upon His chosen Prophet, the one with great moral character; and upon his progeny, his companions, those who followed his path, and those who were guided by his message until the day we shall stand in front of You, O Lord of the Worlds.

To proceed, the subject of high moral character is one of great importance in the life of a Muslim, since the Prophet Muhammad ﷺ himself said it was the very purpose of his mission: "Indeed, I was only sent so that I may perfect moral character."[2]

It is necessary for those who believe in the Muhammadan message to adorn themselves entirely with the hue of

2 Mālik, *al-Muwaṭṭā*, 1614.

nobility, with the hue that was the very purpose of Prophethood. It was due to this wonder that we saw an incredible transformation in the conditions of people who abandoned polytheism, disbelief, ignorance, pride, aggressiveness, oppression and murder for a state of generosity, dignity, moral excellence, courtesy, benevolence, humility, mercy and compassion.

The situation was as described by Allah: ﴾*And remember the favour of Allah upon you—when you were enemies, He brought your hearts together, so that you become brothers, by His Grace*﴿ (*Āl-ʿImrān*, 3:103) and He said regarding the sending of His Prophet: ﴾*Allah has conferred a great favour upon the believers by sending amongst them a Messenger who was amongst them, who recites upon them His verses, purifying them, and teaching them The Book and Wisdom—before that, they had been in manifest error*﴿ (*Āl-ʿImrān*, 3:164).

And after their manifest error, He said: ﴾*You are the best of nations brought forth for the people*﴿ (*Āl-ʿImrān*, 3:110). With goodness, they came; and with goodness, they taught various nations and guided them. Amongst them were heroes, leaders, people of vast learning and gnosis, and paragons of piety and virtue. The essence of this message spread amongst them so they transformed from one state to a far, far loftier one.

Since you believe in Allah and His Messenger, it is only right that you ponder upon this immense message and contemplate on how its deeper meanings may enter your heart. You must introspect as to how your faith manifests itself in your words, deeds and speech. You will notice that Allah mentions faith alongside good deeds in many verses of His Book—giving glad tidings from Him to those who have faith and do good, promising them honour and grace.

You need to reflect upon yourself and the degree to which you have received and appropriated this Prophetic Message. Indeed, dear believer, you are recognised by your exemplary character.

Those who preoccupied themselves with the station of Excellence (*iḥsān*) were called "Sufis" by people in previous centuries. One of them said: "Indeed, our path and our Sufism is just noble character, so whoever surpasses you in character has surpassed you on the spiritual path and surpassed you in rank." Thus, the essence of Sufism is nothing more than the noble character which the Prophet was sent with.

So reflect upon your character in your dealings with people and try hard to acquire virtuous traits. Free and purify yourself from lowly mannerisms which are despised by your Lord and His Prophet. Seek the pleasure of Allah by acquiring these praiseworthy traits for "Indeed, a man attains the rank of the one who fasts and stands in prayer [at night] does so by virtue of his good character."[3] Just by adopting good character, you are able to attain the rank of one who is engaged in worship day and night.

The Prophet ﷺ said: "There is nothing that weighs heavier upon the scales when placed than good character."[4] It has been narrated from al-Ḥasan, who narrates from al-Ḥasan, who narrates from al-Ḥasan, who narrates from Abū al-Ḥasan [i.e., ʿAlī ibn Abī Ṭālib] who narrates from the grandfather of al-Hasan [i.e. the Prophet Muhammad]: "The most excellent of good (*aḥsan al-ḥasan*) is good character (*al-khuluq al-ḥasan*)."[5]

Good character is a garment which Allah adorns upon His chosen servants. The Prophet ﷺ said: "Allah does not beautify a person's physical form and character and then

3 Abū Dāwūd, 4798.
4 Tirmidhī, 2002.
5 Suyūṭī, *al-Jāmiʿ al-ṣaghīr*, 2183.

let the Fire consume him."[6] When a person betters their inner-self, the Fire will not be able to consume and touch them.

Therefore, we should occupy ourselves with obtaining good character and reflect upon the lessons relayed to us. Strive to perfect your character as much as possible as well as your dealings with people. Show mercy and compassion to the creation so that you may be shown mercy and compassion by Allah. Indeed, reward is only granted in accordance with the action.

The Prophet ﷺ narrates to us a story about an Israelite man who was a wealthy businessman. He would often say to his debt collectors: "Go to the wealthy man and allow him time to pay his debt back. Do not rush him at all. As for the poor man who owes us, overlook his debt so that Allah may overlook our wrongdoings." When he died, Allah raised the man and asked him: "What did you used to do?" He said: "O Lord! I would say to my debt collectors: 'Allow the wealthy man time to pay his debt back and overlook the poor man so that Allah may overlook our wrongdoings." Allah said: "It is right that We are more generous than you, so We have pardoned you."[7] The reward

---

6 Ṭabarānī, *Shuʿab al-Īmān*, 7678.
7 Bukhārī, 2078 & 3450.

for pardoning the slaves of Allah was to be pardoned by Allah Himself.

It has also been narrated that an Israelite woman was once approached by a beggar whilst she was eating. She was just about to eat the last morsel when she saw the beggar, who was starving, so she gave him that last morsel which she was about to eat. Everything seemed normal until a few days later when a wolf approached her. Before she realised it, the wolf snatched her child and went away. She ran after the wolf screaming: "My son! My son!" Suddenly, a man appeared, who grabbed the wolf and took the baby from the clutches of the wolf's mouth. He then returned the baby safe and sound to the mother and said: "I am an angel sent by Allah from the heavens to save this son of yours and return him to you. He says to you: 'A morsel for a morsel. You gave a morsel for the sake of Allah, so we will return this morsel (the child) for that morsel.'"[8] As was said, reward is only granted in accordance with the action.

Strive to be of dignified manners and read aplenty on the conduct of your Prophet ﷺ and his blessed life. Reading these books will strengthen your faith and certitude. It

---

8 Hindī, *Kanz al-ʿUmmāl*, 2183.

will open the door for you to emulate the Messenger and follow his teachings.

O Allah allow us to benefit from what we have heard. Teach us what will benefit us and bless us in this regard.

Send your everlasting salutations upon Your Chosen One, Muhammad, and upon his progeny, his companions, Your Prophets, Your Messengers, Your Angels, and Your pious servants.

Send blessings upon us for their sake with Your Mercy, O Most Merciful One. And all Praise be to Allah, Lord of the Worlds.

## One

عَنْ عائِشَةَ ﵂، أُمِّ الْمُؤمِنِيْنَ قالَتْ: كانَ خُلُقُهُ القُرآنَ.

رَوَاهُ الْإِمَامُ أَحْمَدُ وَمُسْلِمُ وَأَبُو دَاوُدَ.

The Mother of the Believers, Lady ʿĀ'ishah ﵂, said: **"His character was the Qur'an."**

Narrated by Imam Aḥmad, Muslim, and Abū Dāwūd.[9]

**Commentary**: The Qur'an is the final Divine Book revealed by Allah to Prophet Muhammad ﷺ for the guidance of all mankind. The Prophet Muhammad ﷺ, being the noblest and esteemed of all Prophets, was chosen by Allah to be the recipient and, as such, was a physical and spiritual embodiment of Qur'anic guidance.

The Qur'an is the Word of Allah. As such, it is a timeless Book ﴾*in which there is no doubt*﴿ (*al-Baqarah*, 2:2). Its oceanic depths know no bound, for it is peerless in its eloquence,

9 Aḥmad, 24601; Muslim, 746; Abū Dāwūd, 1342.

rhetoric, and rhyming prose (*sajʿ*)—containing within it infinite pearls of meanings, guidance, and mysteries.

Other Divine Books were revealed to other Prophets, such as the Torah and Gospel being revealed to Prophet Moses and Prophet Jesus, respectively, but they were all abrogated with the revelation of the Qur'an.

The Qur'an challenges those who question its veracity to bring forth a single chapter like that in the Qur'an if they are able to do so; the challenge is further revised—asking the men and Jinn to join together to bring a single verse like it.

There have been many books written by Islamic scholars on the inimitability of the Qur'an and its excellence. So how better to describe the character of the Prophet Muhammad ﷺ than to liken it to the Qur'an?

Murtaḍā al-Zabīdī writes: "[His character is like the Qur'an means that he would guide towards] all that the Qur'an indicates in terms of the commands, prohibitions, promises, threats, etc."[10] Al-Qāḍī ʿIyāḍ al-Mālikī writes: "His character was all that is detailed in the Qur'an."[11]

Even non-believers who read the Qur'an without the lens of prejudice are forced to accept its brilliance. In fact, many accepted the truth upon hearing the Divine Word such as the second Caliph, ʿUmar ibn al-Khaṭṭāb.

---

10 Zabīdī, *Itḥāf al-Sādah*, 7:92.

11 Ibid.

Johann Wolfgang von Goethe, the German playwright and poet, writes in his *West–östlicher Divan*: "In compliance with the content and purpose of the Qur'an, the style is austere, grand, fearsome, and in places truly sublime.[12] Thus, one nail drives another, and no one should wonder about the great impact of this book."[13]

Muslims should therefore try to read the Qur'an as much as possible, ideally alongside a translation and commentary, so that they may follow the way shown by the Prophet Muhammad ﷺ. They should refer to the explanations of traditional scholars with the intention of adhering to Allah's commands, desisting from that which He has prohibited, and modelling themselves after the righteous ones mentioned in the Qur'an.

---

12 The phrase "truly sublime" was a superlative used to describe the parts that deeply moved Goethe. Dr Katharina Mommsen, an expert on his literary works, writes: "If one is acquainted with Goethe's way of expression, one knows that the words 'truly sublime' belong to the highest attributes which he could assign to a literary landmark." [*The Muslim*, p. 16].

13 Goethe, *West-East Divan: Poems, with "Notes and Essays"*, p. 192.

## *Two*

عَنْ اَنَسٍ رضي الله عنه قالَ: كانَ رَسُوْلُ اللهِ ﷺ أحسَنَ النّاسِ، وأجْوَدَ النّاسِ، وأشْجَعَ النّاسِ.

رَوَاهُ الْبُخَارِيُّ وَمُسْلِمُ وَالتِّرْمِذِيُّ وَابْنُ مَاجَهْ.

Anas [ibn Mālik] رضي الله عنه said: "**The Messenger of Allah ﷺ was the most excellent of people, the most generous of people, and the most courageous of people.**"

Narrated by al-Bukhārī, Muslim, al-Tirmidhī, and Ibn Mājah.[14]

**Commentary**: The Prophet ﷺ was the most excellent in every aspect: in his external form and character, in his lineage and ancestry, in his social conduct, companionship, and in all other praiseworthy traits.

14 Bukhārī, 2820; Muslim, 2307; Tirmidhī, 1687; Ibn Mājah, 2772.

*How grand the form of a Prophet brightened by character,*
*Enveloped by handsomeness, distinguished by jollity!*
*Like flowers in fineness, the full Moon in nobility,*
*The ocean in giving, and time in all tenacity.*[15]

His Companions and those close to him mention that he was the most kind, most generous, and most softly-spoken of all people. He would remind them to be gentle to their family and children, to orphans and widows, and to be generous to the poor and even animals. And in matters concerning the truth, there he was, the most just and fearless of all. Truly, our feeble minds are incapable of comprehending the vastness of his blessed personality.

Only those who saw him and experienced his presence first-hand would come close to knowing the greatness of his character. Those closest to him were the most captivated by him. We can only imagine how sublime his company was—akin to those who are left to read the description of a beautiful rose compared to someone who is fortunate enough to see it, feel it and experience its fragrance.

Only those who saw him and felt his presence first-hand would truly know and comprehend the greatness of his character; we can only imagine how sublime his company was—similar to looking at the picture of a beautiful rose or

---

15 Būṣīrī.

reading its description, compared to someone who has seen, felt and experienced its fragrance.

ʿAlī ibn Abī Ṭālib, the fourth caliph in Islam, who was famous for his bravery and skill on the battlefield once said recalling the courage of the Prophet ﷺ: "You have seen us in the Battle of Badr. We were there, rallying behind the Prophet ﷺ, seeking his protection. In that battle, he ﷺ was at the forefront and the closest to the enemy. He was the most valiant and fearless of all people on that day."[16]

This is also evidence of the truthfulness of the Prophet ﷺ. He ﷺ was a brave and courageous leader, one who was at the forefront—not someone who would stay behind and let his Companions fight on his behalf. In fact, the Companions would consider those who stood closest to him as the bravest and most courageous among them.[17]

We have learned of his valour and bravery. Now let us take a look at another aspect of his noble character. Once, the companions burnt an anthill on their way on a journey. When he ﷺ came to know of this, he was angry at them and forbade them from doing so in the future. In another incident, a companion took away the little ones of a bird—the Prophet ﷺ asked him to return it and told him not to cause distress to the bird.[18]

---

16 Aṣbahānī, *Akhlāq al-Nabī wa Ādābuh,* (1:313) 103.
17 Muslim, 1776.
18 Abū Dāwūd, 2675.

He ﷺ emphasised being mindful and compassionate towards every living being, saying: "The reward of charity is attained by helping every creature with a moist liver."[19]

*In a gathering of friends—soft like silk, yet*
*In the battle between truth and false, the believer is a warrior!*[20]

## *Three*

عَنْ أَنَسِ بْنِ مَالِكٍ ؓ قَالَ: كَانَ رَسُوْلُ اللهِ ﷺ أَحْسَنَ النَّاسِ خُلُقًا.

Anas [ibn Mālik] ؓ said: **"The Messenger of Allah ﷺ was the best of all people in character."**[21]

**Commentary**: Allah says in the Qur'an: ﴾*And indeed you are of excellent character*﴿ (*al-Qalam*, 68:4). And the Prophet ﷺ himself said: "I was only sent to perfect excellent character."[22] Thus, one of the missions of the Prophet ﷺ was to perfect

19 Bukhārī, 6009; Muslim, 2244.
20 Iqbāl.
21 Bukhārī, 6203; Muslim, 2310; Aḥmad, 13209; Bayhaqī, *Dalā'il al-Nubuwwah*, 1:313.
22 Mālik, *al-Muwaṭṭā*, 1614.

noble character and teach it to the people; we see its practical application in the life of the Prophet ﷺ himself.

It is often said: "Judge a man, not on how he treats his equals but those lower than him." It is commonly seen that people humble themselves to their superiors or treat their peers with respect whilst being derisive and overbearing towards those whom they consider 'beneath' them.

Here, it is none other than the servant of the Prophet Muhammad ﷺ, Anas ibn Mālik, who has testified to his impeccable character. He mentions in another narration: "I served the Prophet Muhammad ﷺ for ten years. He never once said 'fie' to me, nor did he say, 'Why did you do this?' or 'Why did you not do that?'"[23]

It was this sublime character of the Prophet Muhammad ﷺ which transformed an entire nation known for bloodshed, superstition and harshness into among the best of those who walked this Earth. They were blessed with the company of the Chosen one—becoming completely devoted to him and sacrificing everything for him readily. They were prepared to fight for him, give up their wealth, family and ultimately their own lives all for his sake.

People blinded by their bigotry say that Islam was spread by violence and the sword. Stanley Lane-Poole, the 19th-century archaeologist and orientalist, responds to this: "Some have

---

23 Bukhārī, 6038.

attempted to explain the first overwhelming success of Islam by the argument of the sword. They forget Carlyle's laconic reply, 'First get your sword.' You must win men's hearts before you can induce them to imperil their lives for you."[24]

He ﷺ won the hearts of people and those who became his Companions were captivated by him. This love and devotion did not end with his Companions. Each successive generation of Muslims continued to adore him and follow his example. Billions of hearts continue to beat for him to this very day.

## *Four*

عَنْ أَبِي سَعِيدٍ الْخُدْرِيِّ رضي الله عنه يَقُولُ: كانَ رَسُوْلُ اللهِ ﷺ أَشَدَّ حَيَاءً مِنَ الْعَذْرَاءِ فِي خِدْرِهَا.

رَوَاهُ الْإِمَامُ أَحْمَدُ وَالْبُخَارِيُّ وَمُسْلِمُ وَابْنُ مَاجَهْ.

Abū Saʿīd al-Khudrī رضي الله عنه said: "**The Messenger of Allah ﷺ was more modest than a virgin in her chambers.**"

Narrated by Imam Aḥmad, al-Bukhārī, Muslim, and Ibn Mājah.[25]

---

24 Lane-Poole, *Studies in a Mosque*, pp. 86-87.

25 Aḥmad, 11683; Bukhārī, 6119; Muslim, 2320; Ibn Mājah, 4180.

**Commentary**: Shyness and bashfulness, known collectively as *ḥayā'* (modesty), are hallmarks of Islam and Muslims. *Ḥayā'* is an attribute which differentiates Islam from all other religions as per the words of the Prophet Muhammad ﷺ: "Every religion has a defining character trait, and the defining character trait of this religion is modesty."[26]

*Ḥayā'* is an existential humility before the Creator that the Prophet ﷺ exhibited in all moments, for the one who is constantly in remembrance and mindful of the Lord is too bashful to disobey Him insolently.

Shyness ought not to be mistaken for timidity or lack of courage. We have already learnt that the Messenger of Allah ﷺ was the bravest and most courageous of all people. Yet, he was also from amongst the most bashful and shy. Imam Ibrāhīm al-Bājūrī, the Shaykh of the Al-Azhar University in the 19th century, writes: "Shyness is a praiseworthy trait so long as it does not lead to weakness, cowardice, moving away from the truth, or failing to establish Islamic penalties. If shyness leads to the above, then it becomes blameworthy."[27]

In modern society, shamelessness and debauchery are celebrated; hedonism is rife, brazenness and impudence are glorified. A Muslim should follow the example of the Prophet

26 Ibn Mājah, 4182.

27 Bājūrī, *al-Mawāhib al-Ladunniyyah*, (p. 602) 358.

ﷺ rather than be influenced by traits that are reprehensible and contrary to human nature.

### *Five*

عَنْ عائِشَةَ ؓ قالَتْ: كانَ رَسُوْلُ اللهِ ﷺ إذا خَلا بِنِسائِهِ أَلْيَنَ النّاسِ وَأَكْرَمَ النّاسِ ضاحِكاً بَسّامًا.

رَوَاهُ ابْنُ سَعْدٍ، وَابْنُ عَسَاكِرْ.

Lady ʿĀ'ishah ؓ said: **"When the Messenger of Allah ﷺ was alone with his wives, he was the most delicate of all people and the most kind-hearted of all people; always smiling and cheerful."**

Narrated by Ibn Saʿd and Ibn ʿAsākir.[28]

**Commentary**: *Layyin*, the word mentioned in the hadith, refers to gentleness, a certain softness and easygoing nature, free from harshness—whether in speech or action. Throughout history, in various cultures and locations, women have been unjustly treated as second-class people, if not outright disregarded as individuals entirely.

28 Ibn Saʿd, *al-Ṭabaqāt al-Kabīr*, 1:314; Ibn ʿAsākir, *Tārīkh Madīnah al-Dimashq*, 3:383.

It was the Prophet Muhammad ﷺ who, over 1400 years ago, showed mankind how to treat women with consideration, love and respect. Islamophobic narratives paint a terrifying picture of an oppressed Muslim woman in a veil—whereas the Prophet ﷺ advised his followers to behave with women in a kind and courteous manner until his last breath: "I advise you to treat women well"[29] and "The best amongst you are the ones who are best towards their women."[30]

Another common trope pushed is that of the 'oppressive religious folk', but religiosity does not mean being self-centred and brash. Allah says about the Prophet ﷺ: ﴾*It is due to Allah's mercy that you are gentle with them. Had you been harsh and hard-hearted, they would have dispersed from you*﴿ (*Āl-ʿImrān*, 3:159).

As such, he ﷺ was gentle with people but in particular with his wives. Being the Perfect Man, he was mindful of fulfilling each and every one of his duties and obligations. Alphonse de Lamartine, the French poet and statesman writes: "Orator, apostle, lawgiver, warrior, conqueror of ideas, restorer of rational dogmas, of a worship without images; the founder of twenty terrestrial empires and of one spiritual empire—that is Muhammad ﷺ. What man was greater, by all the scales on which we measure human greatness?"[31]

29 Bukhārī, 3153.
30 Tirmidhī, 1162.
31 Lamartine, *History of Turkey*, p. 155.

Whilst the above quote of Lamartine captures some of the public and political achievements of the Prophet ﷺ, it does not mention the private and personal sphere of his life. The Prophet Muhammad ﷺ was an intimate friend, husband, father, tradesman, supporter of the poor and guardian of the downtrodden. In all facets of life that a human can endeavour to excel in, we find him as the paradigm of perfection.

Despite suffering intense hardship and persecution by the non-believers, this never led to harshness in his personality. Rather, he ﷺ was always patient, gentle, and caring. He would joke with his Companions and his wives, making them feel comfortable in his presence, and demonstrating to them how to be balanced human beings. He would however caution them to avoid excessive joking, reminding them of both the Mercy of the Lord as well as His Just Might: "If you knew what I knew, you would laugh less and cry more."[32]

32 Muslim, 2359.

## Six

عَنْ عائِشَةَ رضي الله عنها قالَتْ: كانَ رَسُوْلُ اللهِ ﷺ إذا دَخَلَ، قالَ: هَلْ عِنْدَكُمْ طَعَامٌ؟ فَإِذا قِيْلَ: لا، قالَ: إِنِّيْ صائِمٌ.

رَوَاهُ أَبُو دَاوُدَ.

Lady ʿĀʾishah رضي الله عنها said: **"When the Prophet ﷺ entered, he would ask: 'Do you have anything to eat?' If he was told 'No', he ﷺ would say:** '[Then] **I will fast.'"**

Narrated by Abū Dāwūd.[33]

**Comments:** The Prophet Muhammad ﷺ said, "The believer's state is a marvel. If he is granted goodness, he praises Allah. If he suffers adversity, he praises Allah and is patient."[34]

The Prophet ﷺ adopted a frugal and simple lifestyle. If he so desired, he could have relished in the most exquisite and rarest of delicacies, which would have been coveted by even the most powerful of rulers. Instead, he chose to live a life shunning luxuries and opulence. This was to show the believers how to be grateful and patient in their own lives, not becoming ensnared by the temptations of the world.

---

33 Abū Dāwūd, 2455.

34 Aḥmad, 1492.

ʿAbd al-Ra'ūf al-Munāwī, a prolific 16th-century Cairene scholar, says that this narration demonstrates the Prophet's ﷺ contentment. If there was food present, he would eat. If not, he would observe a voluntary fast instead.[35]

The Prophet's ﷺ wife, Lady ʿĀ'ishah ؓ, mentions: "We, the Family of Muhammad ﷺ, would go an entire month without lighting a fire [to cook food with]. There would only be dates and water to consume."[36] In another narration, the Prophet ﷺ himself said: "Thirty consecutive days and nights passed, and there was no food for Bilāl and I to eat except for some food that he carried under his arm."[37]

On one occasion, some companions complained to the Prophet ﷺ of their hunger and lifted their upper garments to show him the stones tied to their stomachs[38] in order to reduce the pangs of hunger. The Prophet ﷺ then lifted his blessed shirt to show them he had two stones tied over his stomach due to his hunger.[39]

---

35 Munāwī, *Fayḍ al-Qadīr*, (5:166) 6675.

36 Muslim, 2972.

37 Tirmidhī, 2472.

38 This is a process known as 'stomach-binding.' A stone is tied over the stomach when one is extremely hungry and cannot stand upright to reduce the pangs of hunger.

39 Tirmidhī, 2371.

*And out of hunger he tied a stone over his abdomen*
*And tightened it; beneath was his delicate skin, so velvety.*[40]

The fasting of Prophet Muhammad ﷺ was a form of devotion, yet even when he did not partake in fasting, his consumption of food—little as it was—was still an act of worship for it was done with gratitude and a pure intention. In all circumstances, the Prophet ﷺ exemplified the utmost devotion to Allah. Likewise, Muslims are advised to make the best of whatever life presents. Contentment with Allah's Decree is spiritual elixir.

## *Seven*

عَنْ كَعْبِ بْنِ مَالِكٍ رضي الله عنه قالَ: كَانَ رَسُوْلُ اللهِ ﷺ إِذَا سُرَّ اسْتَنَارَ وَجْهُهُ كَأَنَّ وَجْهَهُ قِطْعَةُ قَمَرٍ.

رَوَاهُ الْبُخَارِيُّ وَمُسْلِمٌ.

Kaʿb ibn Mālik رضي الله عنه said: **"When the Prophet ﷺ was happy, his face would light up as if it were a piece of the Moon."**

40 Būṣīrī.

Narrated by al-Bukhārī and Muslim.[41]

**Commentary:** Prophet Muhammad ﷺ had a mission to cleanse and purify the heart and soul of humanity. Allah says: ﴾*We have not sent you except as a mercy for all worlds*﴿ (*al-Anbiyā*, 21:107).

When he ﷺ was happy, he would beam with joy. Like a ray of sunshine, that falls in a dark room and basks it in light—the Prophet's ﷺ happiness would lighten up and warm the hearts of everyone around him. The Prophet's ﷺ beautiful countenance and a smiling face was a sight to behold. No wonder, the companion described it as "a piece of the Moon."

Ibn Ḥajar al-ʿAsqalānī noted: "And perhaps by 'piece (*qiṭʿah*) of the Moon', he meant the Moon itself."[42] This is because the Prophet's ﷺ beauty eclipsed the beauty of the full Moon in all of its glory as attested to by his Companions.

Jābir ibn Samurah said: "I saw the Messenger of Allah ﷺ on a moonlit night and he was wearing a reddish cloak. I started looking at him and then at the Moon. For me, he was undoubtedly more beautiful than the full Moon."[43]

When the Creator of the world has praised him, our tongues are futile in comparison. Here, we will suffice with the following verse:

---

41 Bukhārī, 3556; Muslim, 2769.

42 ʿAsqalānī, *Fatḥ al-Bārī*, 10:422.

43 Tirmidhī, 2811.

*O ye of immense beauty, O king of mankind*
*From your luminous face, does the Moon receive its shine*
*It is not possible to praise you as you ought to be praised—*
*In short, all that can be said is: After God, you are the greatest.*[44]

## Eight

عَنْ أَنَسِ بْنِ مَالِكٍ رضي الله عنه قَالَ: كَانَ رَسُوْلُ اللهِ ﷺ إِذَا صَلَّى الْغَدَاةَ جَاءَ خَدَمُ الْمَدِينَةِ بِآنِيَتِهِمْ فِيهَا الْمَاءُ، فَمَا يُؤْتَى بِإِنَاءٍ إِلَّا غَمَسَ يَدَهُ فِيهَا.

رَوَاهُ الْإِمَامُ أَحْمَدُ وَمُسْلِمٌ.

Anas ibn Mālik رضي الله عنه said: **"When the Messenger of Allah ﷺ finished his morning prayer, some servants of Madīnah came to him with their containers filled with water. No container was brought to him except he would dip his hands in it."**

Narrated by Imam Aḥmad and Muslim.[45]

44 This verse is often attributed to 'Abd al-Ḥaqq al-Dihlawī.
45 Aḥmad, 12401; Muslim, 2324.

**Commentary:** Muslims believe in spiritual blessings. It is no surprise then that the Companions would rush to the Prophet ﷺ to attain these ethereal blessings for themselves.

Imam Yaḥyā ibn Sharaf al-Nawawī writes: "This narration and others point towards the Prophet's ﷺ accessibility and closeness with the people. This was so that people may have their rights upheld through his mediation, and so that those unaware of religious etiquettes may imitate him by observation and learning from his actions and movements. This is how leaders should behave. It also shows his patience upon hardship which he ﷺ willingly undertook for the benefit of others, as well as his acceding to people's requests to bless them by placing his hands over [their containers] or by placing them in water, as is mentioned."[46]

Interestingly, it was not the noblemen and wealthy merchants for whom the Prophet ﷺ patiently stood in order to bless each and every one of them. Rather, it was the poor and destitute servants that he ﷺ was tending to—those overlooked and mistreated by others. In his majestic presence, they were shown nothing but honour and respect. After all, as mentioned, he was sent as ﴾*a mercy for all worlds*﴿ (*al-Anbiyā*, 21:107).

It is easy and expedient to respect the rich, powerful and influential in society because we stand to gain something, even

---

46 Nawawī, *al-Minhāj fī Sharḥ Ṣaḥīḥ Muslim*, 15:119.

if it is just good will. Yet, we frown and disregard those who are less fortunate, those who may be less in worldly standing but high in their standing with the Lord. We should all strive to emulate this trait of his and honour those who may be frowned upon by society, yet may be carrying the wealth of spirituality and closeness to Allah in their hearts.

## *Nine*

عَنِ ابْنِ عُمَرَ رضي الله عنه قَالَ: كَانَ رَسُوْلُ اللهِ ﷺ إِذَا صَلَّى بِالنَّاسِ الْغَدَاةَ أَقْبَلَ عَلَيْهِمْ بِوَجْهِهِ، فَقَالَ: هَلْ فِيكُمْ جِنَازَةٌ أَتْبَعُهَا؟ فَإِنْ قَالُوا: لَا، قَالَ: مَنْ رَأَى مِنْكُمْ رُؤْيَا يَقُصُّهَا عَلَيْنَا.

رَوَاهُ ابْنُ عَسَاكِرٍ.

[ʿAbd-Allāh] ibn ʿUmar رضي الله عنه said: **"When the Messenger of Allah ﷺ would finish leading the morning prayer, he would turn to the people and ask: 'Is there a funeral amongst you that I should partake in?' If the people said "No", he would ask: 'Who amongst you has seen a dream which they will relate to us?'"**

Narrated by Ibn ʿAsākir.[47]

47 Ibn ʿAsākir, *Tārīkh Madīnah al-Dimashq*, 39:114.

**Commentary:** Whenever his Companions would seek his assistance, he ﷺ would readily say: "I am present!"[48] For he was not one who was aloof from the people. Immediately after completing the morning prayer, he would face his Companions and ask how he could be of service to them—whether by attending a funeral, answering their queries, or interpreting their dreams.

This sensitivity of the Prophet Muhammad ﷺ towards people demonstrates his softness of heart and affection. While kings and other leaders require extravagant protocol to meet them, it was the Prophet ﷺ himself who would attend to his congregants.

He was the Master. He was their leader and they were his people. It is not uncommon for followers to have a deep reverence for their leader, yet this sentiment is not always reciprocated. However, with the Prophet ﷺ he displayed a remarkable level of care and compassion for them.

He was available for everyone; and his turning towards them was a recognition of their individuality. He met everyone and would engage with them, being entirely present. None among his companions was disregarded, overlooked or treated as another face in the crowd.

---

48 *Akhlāq al-Nabī wa Ādābuh*, (1:75) 2.

Al-Munāwī writes: "He ﷺ would turn towards them [after completing the prayer] to encourage them to ask him questions and create an opportunity for them to ask."[49]

We also learn how the Prophet ﷺ was 'a Prophet for the people' — someone who lived amongst them, ate with them and spent time with them. In fact, he said: "The believer who mixes with the people and is patient upon their harm receives greater reward than the believer who does not mix with the people and so is not patient upon their harm."[50] Humans are social creatures, and Islam is a way of life that takes our innate nature into consideration. As such, to isolate oneself unnecessarily is frowned upon.

## *Ten*

عَنْ أَبِي هُرَيْرَةَ رضي الله عنه قالَ: كانَ رَسُوْلُ اللهِ ﷺ إذا عَطَسَ، وَضَعَ يَدَهُ -أَوْ ثَوْبَهُ- عَلى فيهِ، وَخَفَضَ بِها صَوْتَهُ.

رَوَاهُ أَبُو دَاوُدَ وَالتِّرْمِذِيُّ وَالْحَاكِمُ.

Abū Hurayrah رضي الله عنه said: **"When the Messenger of Allah ﷺ sneezed, he would place his hand or his**

49 *Fayḍ al-Qadīr*, (5:186) 6738.
50 Ibn Mājah, 4032.

**garment over his mouth to suppress the sound of his sneeze."**

Narrated by Abū Dāwūd, al-Tirmidhī, and al-Ḥākim.[51]

**Commentary:** This was done out of propriety and good conduct since sneezing loudly is generally considered an annoyance to those nearby. The Prophet ﷺ covering his mouth would teach others how to carry themselves and behave in social settings.

It has also been mentioned that the wisdom behind teaching the Companions to cover their mouths was to ensure that those nearby are not inconvenienced by the mucus that is discharged when sneezing.

Basic hygiene was not given much consideration in pre-Islamic Arabia. In fact, even in 19th-century Europe, bathing and other personal hygiene practices were relatively uncommon. Yet, over 1400 years ago, the Prophet Muhammad ﷺ made it incumbent upon Muslims to wash five times a day, declaring: "Cleanliness is half of faith."[52] Hygienic practices and grooming, therefore, became a part and parcel of Islam—from trimming hair, cutting nails, cleaning oneself after visiting the bathroom, performing ablution, and bathing. It would not

---

51 Abū Dāwūd, 5029; Tirmidhī, 2745; Ḥākim, *Mustadrak*, 7796.
52 Muslim, 223.

be wrong to say that Islam is the religion that taught hygiene to the rest of the world.

Non-believers would taunt the Companions of the Prophet Muhammad ﷺ, saying that: "I hear that your master (i.e., the Prophet ﷺ) teaches you about everything, including going to the bathroom." This was said mockingly because they could not fathom that basic hygiene was important in this faith that was new to them. Salman, the Persian, who was a Christian before accepting Islam, replied: "Yes, that is the case. He prohibited us from facing the Qiblah when relieving ourselves or from cleaning ourselves with our right hands or with less than three pebbles or using dung or bones."[53]

It is this attention to detail and focus on the minutiae of life which makes Islam stand out from other religions. David George Hogarth, the 19th century English archaeologist and Keeper of the Ashmolean Museum in Oxford, writes: "Serious or trivial, his daily behaviour has instituted a canon which millions observe this day with conscious mimicry. No one regarded by any section of the human race as Perfect Man has been imitated so minutely. The conduct of the Founder of Christianity has not so governed the ordinary life of His followers. Moreover, no Founder of a religion has been left on so solitary an eminence as the Muslim Apostle."[54]

---

53 Muslim, 223.

54 Hogarth, *Arabia*, p. 52.

## Eleven

عَنْ أَنَسٍ ﷺ، قَالَ: كَانَ رَسُوْلُ اللهِ ﷺ إِذَا فَقَدَ الرَّجُلَ مِنْ إِخْوَانِهِ ثَلَاثَةَ أَيَّامٍ سَأَلَ عَنْهُ، فَإِنْ كَانَ غَائِبًا دَعَا لَهُ، وَإِنْ كَانَ شَاهِدًا زَارَهُ، وَإِنْ كَانَ مَرِيضًا عَادَهُ.

رَوَاهُ أَبُو يَعْلَى

Anas [ibn Mālik] ﷺ said: **"When the Messenger of Allah ﷺ would not see one of his companions[55] for three days, he would ask about him. If he were away, he would pray for him; if he were present** [in the town], **he would visit him; and if he were sick, he would go and check on him."**

Narrated by Abū Yaʿlā.[56]

**Commentary:** It is revealed in the Qur'an regarding the Prophet's ﷺ feelings towards his companions: ﴿*Your suffering weighs hard upon him; he is anxious for your well-being and kind and merciful to the believers*﴾ (*al-Tawbah*, 9:128). He made everyone around him feel welcome and cherished; so much

55 *Ikhwānihi*, lit. his brothers
56 Abū Yaʿlā, *Musnad*, 3429.

so that each person was convinced that they were the dearest to the Prophet ﷺ.[57]

So we learn the love and devotion the companions had for the Prophet ﷺ is secondary—for their love for him is far eclipsed by his love for them. O what love! He said: "If a believer dies and has a debt, it is for me to settle; and if he has left behind wealth and property, then it is for his heirs."[58]

This genuine care and concern of the Prophet ﷺ for others inspired his companions to emulate him and fostered unbreakable bonds of solidarity and brotherhood. This is also in accordance with the Divine Command: ﴾*Indeed, believers are brothers*﴿ (*al-Ḥujurāt*, 49:10) and has been followed by Muslims literally down the ages. The Prophet's ﷺ words further solidify this: "A believer is a brother of another believer; he does not oppress him, he does not abandon him, he does not humiliate him."[59]

57 Tirmidhī, *al-Shamā'il al-Muḥammadiyyah*, (p. 162) 330.
58 Bukhārī, 2298.
59 Muslim, 2565.

## *Twelve*

عَنْ عَبْدِ اللهِ بْنِ جَعْفَرٍ ﵁ قَالَ: كَانَ رَسُوْلُ اللهِ ﷺ إِذَا قَدِمَ مِنْ سَفَرٍ تَلَقَّى بِصِبْيَانِ أَهْلِ بَيْتِهِ.

رَوَاهُ الْإِمَامُ أَحْمَدُ وَمُسْلِمٌ، وَأَبُو دَاوُدَ.

ʿAbd-Allāh ibn Jaʿfar ﵁ said: **"When the Messenger of Allah ﷺ would return from a journey, he would be greeted by the children of his household."**

Narrated by Imam Aḥmad, Muslim, and Abū Dāwūd.[60]

**Commentary:** The Prophet ﷺ emphasised the importance of loving children. He once kissed his grandson, Ḥasan, when a companion said surprised: "I too have ten children and have never kissed any of them". The Prophet ﷺ looked at him and said: "One who does not show mercy will not receive mercy."[61]

The children rushing to welcome the Prophet ﷺ clearly shows that they would wait for him at the outskirts and were eager to see the one who would bring joy to their hearts and please their spirits. ʿAbd-Allāh ibn Jaʿfar mentions: "When he ﷺ would return from a journey, he would meet me, Ḥasan or Ḥusayn. He would carry one of us in his arms and the other

60 Aḥmad, 1743; Muslim, 2428; Abū Dāwūd, 1027.
61 Bukhārī, 5997.

on his back until we entered the town."[62] Other scholars have mentioned that the hadith refers to his uncle's children (i.e., his younger cousins)[63] or his daughter, Fāṭimah.[64]

We learn that the Prophet ﷺ loved children and they too loved him.

## Thirteen

عَنْ أَنَسٍ رَضِيَ اللهُ عَنْهُ قَالَ: كَانَ رَسُوْلُ اللهِ ﷺ إِذَا كَرِهَ شَيْئًا رُؤِيَ ذَلِكَ فِي وَجْهِهِ.

رَوَاهُ الطَّبَرَانِيُّ فِي الْأَوْسَطِ.

Anas [ibn Mālik] رضي الله عنه said: "**When the Messenger of Allah ﷺ disliked something, it** (i.e. his displeasure) **could be seen in his face.**"

Narrated by al-Ṭabarānī in [*al-Muʿjam*] *al-Awsaṭ*.[65]

**Commentary:** The Prophet Muhammad ﷺ was grace and refinement personified. He would not expressly disapprove of

62 Muslim, 2428.
63 Qārī, *Mirqāt al-Mafātīḥ*, (7:415) 3900.
64 *Fayḍ al-Qadīr*, (5:198) 6772.
65 Ṭabarānī, *al-Muʿjam al-Awsaṭ*, 1853.

something or bluntly point out something he disliked. Instead, it would be visible on his blessed face.

He ﷺ did not want to hurt or embarrass them by pointing out something—the subtle hint of displeasure on his face was enough for someone around him to realise that it was undesirable and thus desist from doing so.

His companions loved and respected him so much that their love and dislike were automatically adjusted to his likes and dislikes. Anas ibn Mālik said: "I once saw the Prophet ﷺ eat gourd, and from that day, gourd became beloved to me."

He would neither be angry nor avenge for his own sake. Lady ʿĀ'ishah says: "I never saw the Prophet ﷺ seek revenge for harm or slight to his august person. However, if the Right of Allah were violated, he would become angry [for the sake of Allah]."

It is said that his happiness and anger could be seen on his face. Munāwī writes: "His face was radiant like the sun and the moon; when he disliked something, it was as if a shadow fell upon it - as if a cloud had passed over the sun. Out of modesty, he would never express his displeasure in words—rather, it would be visible on his face."

This hadith is a good example that demonstrates his formidable character, his legendary capacity to forgive, and his determination to see that the law of Allah is not violated. The Prophet ﷺ taught his followers, leading by example, that one could forgive personal insults but would have to be uncompromising in the Commandments of Allah.

## *Fourteen*

عَنْ أَنَسٍ ﵁ قَالَ: كَانَ رَسُوْلُ اللهِ ﷺ إِذَا لَقِيَهُ أَحَدٌ مِنْ أَصْحَابِهِ فَقَامَ مَعَهُ لَمْ يَنْصَرِفْ حَتَّى يَكُونَ الرَّجُلُ هُوَ الَّذِي يَنْصَرِفُ عَنْهُ، وَإِذَا لَقِيَهُ أَحَدٌ مِنْ أَصْحَابِهِ فَتَنَاوَلَ يَدَهُ نَاوَلَهُ إِيَّاهَا فَلَمْ يَنْزِعْ يَدَهُ مِنْهُ حَتَّى يَكُونَ الرَّجُلُ هُوَ الَّذِي يَنْزِعُ يَدَهُ مِنْهُ، وَإِذَا لَقِيَ أَحَدًا مِنْ أَصْحَابِهِ فَتَنَاوَلَ أُذُنَهُ نَاوَلَهُ إِيَّاهَا ثُمَّ لَمْ يَنْزِعْهَا حَتَّى يَكُونَ الرَّجُلُ هُوَ الَّذِي يَنْزِعُهَا عَنْهَا.

رَوَاهُ ابْنُ سَعْدٍ.

Anas [ibn Mālik] ﵁ said: **"When the Messenger of Allah ﷺ was met by one of his companions [on the path], he would stop—and would not move away until the man would himself leave. If the man held out his hand, he would shake his hand and would not leave his hand until the person would himself let it go. If he met someone among his companions who wanted to tell him something, he would lend**

**his ear and would not move until the person himself** [ended the conversation].”

Narrated by Ibn Saʿd.[66]

**Commentary:** This shows how the Prophet ﷺ would be both physically and emotionally present with his Companions. When he would speak to someone, he would face them with his body and divert all of his attention to them. When they would speak, he would listen carefully. By doing so, he would make the person feel completely acknowledged, irrespective of whether they were poor or rich, of a high social status or a slave. This was his sincerity towards all believers.

We sometimes fail to appreciate aspects of the Prophet's ﷺ meticulous social etiquettes, personality, and character. In today's world, the loss of focus and attention is rife. We find people earnestly trying to maintain focus without glancing at their phone. The focus and attention the Prophet ﷺ gave to those around him is a demonstration of his abundant generosity.

Al-Munāwī writes: “This is one of the great proofs of the perfection and excellence of his character. How could it not be so, when he was one of extraordinary humility? He is the one who said: ‘Behave with the people in an excellent manner.’”

66 Ibn Saʿd, *al-Ṭabaqāt al-Kabīr*, 1:326.

There also seems to be a subtle indication in the mannerism of the Prophet Muhammad ﷺ in not removing his hand until the other person did so—teaching us that believers should always seek to hold on, join hands and keep the grip of love firm; and not to be of those who turn away from one another, fester hatred and sever ties.'"[67]

## Fifteen

عَنْ عَائِشَةَ رضي الله عنها قَالَتْ: كَانَ أَبْغَضُ الْخُلُقِ إِلَى رَسُولِ اللهِ ﷺ الْكَذِبَ.

رَوَاهُ الْبَيْهَقِيُّ

Lady ʿĀ'ishah رضي الله عنها said: **"Lying was the most despicable trait to the Messenger of Allah ﷺ."**

Narrated by al-Bayhaqī.[68]

**Commentary:** The Prophet ﷺ was renowned for his truthfulness. Even before he announced his Prophethood, he was known as "The Trustworthy" (*al-amīn*) and "The Truthful" (*al-ṣādiq*).

When he was young, the Kaaba was being rebuilt and the sacred Black Stone (*al-ḥajar al-aswad*) was set to be placed in

67 *Fayḍ al-Qadīr*, (5:203) 6789.
68 Bayhaqī, *Shuʿab al-Īmān*, 4475.

one of the corners. A disagreement arose among the tribes as to who should have the honour of placing the Sacred Stone there. Eventually, they decided that the first person to enter the mosque next day would decide the matter.

The following day, as everyone was anticipating the first person to enter the mosque—lo and behold, it was the Prophet Muhammad ﷺ. When they saw him, they were overjoyed and said: 'Indeed, he is the trustworthy and we can all agree with his decision.'[69]

And true to their expectation, the Prophet ﷺ found a way for them all to partake such that none of the tribes felt slighted. He spread his cloak on the ground and placed the stone with his own hand on it; he then asked the leader of every tribe to hold the cloak together and carry it to where it was to be placed—he then placed it in with his own hands.

When he ﷺ was commanded by Allah to announce his Prophethood to people, he ascended Mount Ṣafā and asked the non-believing people of Mecca: "If I were to tell you that there is an army behind this valley ready to attack, would you believe me?" They said: "Of course, we have always found you to be honest and truthful."[70]

When Abū Sufyān, a former enemy of the Prophet ﷺ who later became a Muslim, went to the emperor Heraclius, he was

69 Ibn Hishām, *al-Sīrah al-Nabawiyyah*, 1:223-224.
70 Bukhārī, 4971.

asked if the Prophet Muhammad ﷺ ever lied or broke his promise. Despite being a vehement opponent of Islam at that time, he replied that the Prophet ﷺ never lied nor did he ever break his promise.[71]

Ordinarily, a person's enemies will leave no stone unturned to show that person in bad light. They may even resort to defamation and slander. The Prophet's ﷺ truthfulness was so compelling that even his sworn enemies found it difficult to deny.

Thomas Carlyle, a 19th century essayist and philosopher, dismisses the theory that many orientalists held that the Prophet Muhammad ﷺ—Allah forbid—was an imposter: "Our current hypothesis about Mahomet [Muhammad], that he was a scheming Impostor, a Falsehood incarnate, that his religion is a mere mass of quackery and fatuity, begins really to be now untenable to anyone."[72]

He further writes refuting those who suggested that the Prophet ﷺ—Allah forbid—had ulterior motives: "Ambition? What could all Arabia do for this man; with the crown of Greek Heraclius, of Persian Chosroes, and all crowns in the Earth;—what could they all do for him? It was not of the Earth he wanted to hear tell; it was of the Heaven above and of the Hell beneath. All crowns and sovereignties whatsoever, where

---

71 Bukhārī, 7.

72 Carlyle, *On Heroes, Hero-Worship, and the Heroic in History*, p. 52.

would they in a few brief years be? To be Sheikh of Mecca or Arabia, and have a bit of gilt wood[73] put into your hand,—will that be one's salvation? I decidedly think, not."[74]

Honesty is the sign of a believer; honesty in word, honesty in deed, and honesty of mind. The Prophet Muhammad ﷺ once said: "Indeed, truthfulness leads to righteousness and righteousness leads to Paradise. A man continues to tell the truth until he becomes Truthful. Lying leads to wickedness and wickedness leads to Hell. A man lies and keeps lying until he will be written as a liar by Allah."[75]

## *Sixteen*

عَنْ ابْنِ عُمَرَ رضي الله عنه قَالَ: كَانَ رَسُوْلُ اللهِ ﷺ إِذَا وَدَّعَ رَجُلًا أَخَذَ بِيَدِهِ فَلَا يَدَعهَا حَتَّى يَكُونَ الرَّجُلُ هُوَ الَّذِي يَدَعُ يَدَهُ، وَيَقُولُ: أَسْتَوْدِعُ اللهَ دِينَكَ وَأَمَانَتَكَ وَخَوَاتِيمَ عَمَلِكَ.

رَوَاهُ الْإِمَامُ أَحْمَدُ، وَالتِّرْمِذِيُّ، وَالنَّسَائِيُّ، وَابْنُ مَاجَهْ، وَالْحَاكِمُ.

---

73 Giltwood refers to wood that has been gilded or painted with gold. It was a symbol of wealth and luxury.

74 Carlyle, *On Heroes, Hero-Worship, and the Heroic in History*, p. 60.

75 Bukhārī, 6094.

[ʿAbd-Allāh] ibn ʿUmar ﷺ said: **"When the Messenger of Allah ﷺ would bid a man farewell, he would hold their hand and would not let go until the person themselves would let go of their hand first. He would then say: 'I entrust Allah with your religion, your responsibility, and your final deeds.'"**

Narrated by Imam Aḥmad, al-Tirmidhī, al-Nasāʾī, Ibn Mājah and al-Ḥākim.[76]

**Commentary:** Mullā ʿAlī al-Qārī writes: "This is referring to when he ﷺ would bid them farewell on a journey. He would not let go of their hands due to his immense humility and as a way of showing his great love and mercy [for them]."[77]

Supplicating to Allah is an act of worship. We are told to supplicate often, even if it is for a shoestring when broken.[78] Likewise, one of the most selfless acts a person can do is to wish good for his fellow believers. What is more beautiful than praying for another from the depths of one's heart, wishing nothing but the best for them?

See comments on hadith fourteen.

---

76 Aḥmad, 4524; Tirmidhī, 3443; Nasāʾī, *al-Sunan al-Kubrā*, 8754; Ibn Mājah, 2826, with the latter part; *al-Mustadrak*, 2475, with the latter part.

77 *Mirqāt al-mafātīḥ*, (5:347) 2435.

78 Tirmidhī, 3973.

## *Seventeen*

عَنْ أَنَسٍ ﷺ قَالَ: كَانَ رَسُوْلُ اللهِ ﷺ أَرْحَمَ النَّاسِ بِالصِّبْيَانِ وَالْعِيَالِ.

رَوَاهُ ابْنُ عَسَاكِرْ.

Anas [ibn Mālik] ﷺ said: **"The Messenger of Allah ﷺ was the most compassionate person towards children and his Household."**

Narrated by Ibn ʿAsākir.[79]

**Commentary:** Some commentators have written that Household (*ʿiyāl*) is referring to the children of the Household in particular; it is also possible that it refers to family members in general. The Prophet ﷺ said: "The best of you are those who are best to your family, and I am the best to my family."[80]

It is important that parents and guardians fulfil their duties in raising children in a proper manner, inculcating Islamic ethics and morals in them. They should not physically or verbally abuse them since this can psychologically scar them.

Likewise, it is also important that they do not emotionally neglect them—by ignoring their needs or by spoiling them

---

79 Ibn ʿAsākir, *Tārīkh Madīnah al-Dimashq*, 4:88.
80 Tirmidhī, 3895.

with excessive admiration or with material gifts. No amount of money or presents can ever compensate for the gift of morality and spirituality. It is important to strike a balance between strict discipline and lenient compassion.

Children are impressionable, so a person must speak and behave diligently around them. The habits they form will harden into character and behaviours that will be very difficult to change once they are older. In extreme cases, poor parenting can even lead to mental health issues and personality disorders such as depression or narcissitic personality disorder, which are difficult to treat and will likely plague the children their entire lives.

Thus, one should cultivate a healthy home environment as much as possible. In spite of commitments and pressures of daily life, the parents should make time for their family. Not only do they have material responsibilities to fulfill but it is even more essential thay they attend to their spiritual needs. What value does this life have if one does not have faith?

## Eighteen

عَنْ أَنَسٍ ﷺ قَالَ: كَانَ رَسُوْلُ اللهِ ﷺ رَحِيمًا، وَكَانَ لَا يَأْتِيهِ أَحَدٌ إِلَّا وَعَدَهُ وَأَنْجَزَ لَهُ إِنْ كَانَ عِنْدَهُ.

رَوَاهُ الْبُخَارِيُّ فِي الْأَدَبِ الْمُفْرَدِ.

Anas [ibn Mālik] ﷺ said: **"The Messenger of Allah ﷺ was very compassionate. None would come to him except he would promise them something and would fulfil it if he had it."**

Narrated by al-Bukhārī in *al-Adab al-Mufrad*.[81]

**Commentary**: In the generosity of the Prophet ﷺ, we see a manifestion of Allah's Magnanimity. Generous people give when they have money, but Prophet ﷺ was so generous that he would not only give when he had, but even when he didn't. A man once asked the Prophet ﷺ for money and he did not have it. So he told the person to take it from someone else in his name and he would settle the debt later.

He ﷺ was the epitome of selflessness and always gave preference to others; and he always relied upon his Lord-Sustainer, the Almighty.

---

81 Bukhārī, *al-Adab al-Mufrad*, 278.

Al-Bājūrī writes: "He ﷺ once granted a person livestock which spanned the space between two mountains. The person returned to his tribe and said: 'Accept Islam for Muhammad ﷺ gives like a man who does not fear poverty.' On another occasion, he was given ninety-thousand Dirhams and he placed it on the mosque floor and divided it, and nobody was refused [any money] on that day."[82]

He always fulfilled his promises. The enemies of the Prophet ﷺ tried to take advantage of his noble trait on one occasion—they entrusted their possessions to him along with other Meccans who would give him various things for safekeeping. They knew that he would not leave without returning their property; and so they were convinced that he was present in his house when they surrounded it to assassinate him. But instead, the Prophet ﷺ entrusted all these to his cousin, ʿAlī - knowing that they would not harm him. ʿAlī then returned them after the Prophet ﷺ had emigrated.

John Adair, an acclaimed leadership theorist, writes: "Clearly, then, Muhammad was a man with a reputation for integrity. That word, from the Latin integer whole, is especially appropriate for Muhammad as far as Muslims are concerned, for in its primary meaning, integrity implies unity that indicates interdependence of the parts and completeness and perfection

82 *Al-Mawāhib al-Ladunniyyah,* (p. 595) 353.

of the whole. Human beings are like stones, some Muslims say, and Muhammad is as the only ruby among them.

Honesty means a refusal to lie, steal, or cheat in any way. Integrity goes a mile beyond honesty: it implies trustworthiness and incorruptibility to a degree that one is incapable of being false to a trust, responsibility, or pledge. A leader with integrity is like the English poet William Wordsworth's "Happy Warrior":

*'Who comprehends his trust, and to the same*
*Keeps faithful, with singleness of aim;*
*And therefore does not stop, nor lie in wait*
*For wealth or honour, or for worldly state.'"*[83]

## Nineteen

عَنْ أَبِي أُمَامَةَ ﵁ قَالَ: كَانَ رَسُوْلُ اللهِ ﷺ مِنْ أَضْحَكِ النَّاسِ وَأَطْيَبِهِمْ نَفْسًا.

رَوَاهُ الطَّبَرَانِيُّ.

Abū Umāmah ﵁ said: **"The Messenger of Allah ﷺ was immensely affable, constantly smiling, and the most pure in personality."**

83 Adair, *The Leadership of Muhammad*, p. 49-50.

Narrated by al-Ṭabarānī.[84]

**Commentary:** This speaks to the Prophet's ﷺ pleasantness. He would always be seen smiling and encouraged his followers to do so as well. "Smiling in the face of your brother is charity."[85] In Islam, charity is not limited to donating monetary goods but rather all good deeds are charitable. A smile is contagious and can spread happiness a long way.

In Arabic, the word for laughter is *ḍaḥik* and the word for smile is *tabassum*. However, the word *ḍaḥik* is inclusive of *tabassum* as it is often reported that the Prophet ﷺ would not laugh. Al-Munāwī writes: "This hadith does not negate other reports stating he would only smile and not laugh. This is because he would smile the majority of the time, and those who narrated regarding him would report about what he would generally do. Each narrator would only report according to what they saw. In the beginning of Islam, he would sometimes laugh until his molars could be seen, whilst towards the end of his life, he would only smile."[86]

See comments on hadith twenty-three.

---

84 Ṭabarānī, *al-Muʿjam al-Kabīr* 7838.
85 Tirmidhī, 1953.
86 *Fayḍ al-Qadīr*, (5:228) 6864.

## *Twenty*

عَنْ أَنَسٍ ﷺ قَالَ: كَانَ رَسُوْلُ اللهِ ﷺ مِنْ أَفْكَهِ النَّاسِ.

رَوَاهُ ابْنُ عَسَاكِرَ.

Anas [ibn Mālik] ﷺ said: **"The Messenger of Allah ﷺ was one of the most cordial of people."**

Narrated by Ibn ʿAsākir.[87]

**Commentary:** The Prophet ﷺ would lift the mood of his Companions and family members by being cheerful and cordial with them—contrary to the common misconception that a practising Muslim must always be morbidly serious. He ﷺ showed us how a person could be contemplative of Allah, their looming death, and the Hereafter whilst also being lighthearted and easygoing.

This is the balance that he ﷺ taught the ﴾*middle nation*﴿ (*al-Baqarah*, 2:143) to uphold. In fact, he mentioned that the most beloved religion to Allah is that which is, "Pure, easy Monotheism."[88] We must be vigilant not to get absorbed by this world, however, we can do this whilst still appreciating

87 *Tārikh Madīnah al-Dimashq*, 4:37.
88 *Al-Adab al-Mufrad*, 287.

the ﴾*favours of Allah*﴿ (*Ibrāhīm*, 14:34), showing gratitude for all He has granted us.

It is mentioned in a hadith that ʿĀ'ishah ﷺ came to the Prophet ﷺ with some porridge. She told Sawdah bint Zamʿah, his other wife, to eat, but she declined. ʿĀ'ishah said: 'If you don't eat it, I will smear it on your face.' But she still refused, so she smeared it on her face. The Prophet ﷺ smiled and told Sawdah: 'Smear her face as well.'[89]

It should be noted that the lightheartedness and playfulness of the Prophet ﷺ was always truthful. He would never lie, even in jest. The Companions said to him: "You are lighthearted with us, O Messenger of Allah ﷺ!" He replied: "Yes, but I only speak the truth."[90]

## *Twenty-One*

عَنْ أَنَسٍ ﷺ عَنْهُ قَالَ: كَانَ رَسُوْلُ اللهِ ﷺ لَا يَأْخُذُ بِالْقَرَفِ وَلَا يَقْبَلُ قَوْلَ أَحَدٍ عَلَى أَحَدٍ.

رَوَاهُ أَبُو نُعَيْمٍ فِي الْحِلْيَةِ.

89 Nasā'ī, *al-Sunan al-Kubrā*, 8868.
90 *Al-Shamā'il al-Muḥammadiyyah*, 238.

Anas [ibn Mālik] ﷺ said: **"The Messenger of Allah ﷺ would not entertain accusations nor would he accept any one person's word over another."**

Narrated by Abū Nuʿaym in *al-Ḥilyah*.[91]

**Commentary:** That is, the Prophet ﷺ was fair and just. He would be the furthest from slander, and nor would he favour one person's word over the other without thoroughly looking into the matter, listening to both sides of the story, and then making an informed decision.

Allah says: ﴾*O you who believe, be upholders of justice—witnesses for Allah, even if it is against yourselves, your parents or kinsmen; be they rich or poor. Allah is a better caretaker for both. So do not follow your desires lest you deviate*﴿ (*al-Nisā*, 4:135).

The above verse implores Muslims to always be just, impartial, and equitable, no matter the consequences. Justice should be upheld even if it be to the detriment of one's friends and family, one's spouse or parents, or even if it be to the detriment of your own selves—for Allah's boundaries supersede all. As we have learnt, the Prophet's ﷺ character was the Qur'an, so it is no surprise that he was the personification of absolute justice and honesty.

---

91 Abū Nuʿaym, *Ḥilyah al-Awliyā'*, 6:310.

It is worth noting that Harvard University, one of the most prestigious institutes of higher education in the world, has written this verse on the entrance wall to its Faculty of Law, recognising it as a powerful embodiment of justice.[92]

In one narration, the Prophet ﷺ said: "Indeed, those who uphold justice will be sat on pulpits of light, considered lofty by their Lord … [they are] those who are just in their rulings, with their families and all that they undertake."[93]

For a believer, pursuing justice in all facets of life is not a mere token gesture but one that should fundamentally direct their lives. We must love and encourage justice and fairness and abhor injustice.

The Prophet ﷺ said: "Whosoever amongst you sees evil, then let him change it by his hand; if not, then with his tongue, and if he is unable to do either, then let him deem it an evil in his heart. And this is the weakest form of faith."[94] That is, the least a person can do is hate the evil or injustice that takes place, if he is unable to make effective change through his actions or speech. One cannot be a true believer, if one is unmoved by injustice and is indifferent towards evil.[95]

---

92 "Which Islamic or Qur'anic Verse or Quote Is Written on Harvard's Main Gate?" Ask a Librarian. Harvard Library. Accessed January 15, 2023. https://ask.library.harvard.edu/faq/82441.

93 Muslim, 1827.

94 Muslim, 8.

95 The scholars have said that rulers and people in positions of authority should 'prevent evil with their hand'; scholars and men of

## *Twenty-Two*

عَنِ ابْنِ عَمْرٍو ﵄ قَالَ: كَانَ رَسُوْلُ اللهِ ﷺ لَا يَأْكُلُ مُتَّكِئًا، وَلَا يَطَأُ عَقِبَهُ رَجُلَانِ.

رَوَاهُ الْإِمَامُ أَحْمَدُ.

[ʿAbd-Allāh] ibn ʿAmr ﵄ said: **"The Messenger of Allah ﷺ would not recline while eating, nor allowed two men to walk behind him."**

Narrated by Imam Aḥmad.[96]

**Commentary:** The Prophet Muhammad ﷺ would sit to eat in a dignified manner. Reclining while eating is the manner of the arrogant, the pompous, and the gluttonous. The Prophet ﷺ himself was the epitome of humility and he taught his followers to be humble. In fact, even the Bible echoes this: "Blessed are the humble, for they shall inherit the earth."[97]

Mullā ʿAlī al-Qārī explains: "He ﷺ would not walk in front of the people, but rather he would walk amongst them or behind them out of humility."[98] For leadership is not about

---

knowledge should 'prevent it with their tongues. The common man should deem it evil and consider it bad in his heart.

96 Aḥmad, 6549; Ibn Mājah, 244; Abū Dāwūd, 3770.

97 Matthew 5:5.

98 *Mirqāt al-Mafātīḥ*, (8:120) 4212.

acting superior and entitled; or forcing followers to be submissive and servile. A real leader does not demand attention, priority and service—whilst he treats them as nobodies.

Great leaders are humble and treat their subordinates with respect. Our master, the greatest leader mankind has known, was the ultimate in this regard; treating his followers with immense care and compassion. The love, respect, allegiance, and loyalty that his followers gave him of their own accord is unimaginable and incredible. Yet, he ﷺ lived amongst them as one of them and refused special treatment.

His companions nonetheless recognised his superiority and would often address him by saying: "May my father and mother be sacrificed for you, O Messenger of Allah ﷺ ..." These were not mere words but rather, a reality which they lived. In a famous incident, a lady lost her husband, father and sons in a battle and yet she was told about them—the only thing she kept asking was: "How is the Messenger of Allah ﷺ?" When she was told that he was safe, she was still not satisfied. It was only when she saw him with her own eyes that her heart felt peace, and she said: "Nothing is lost so long as you are safe!"[99]

---

99 *Dalāʾil al-Nubuwwah*, 3:302.

## *Twenty-Three*

عَنْ أَبِي الدَّرْدَاءِ ﵁ قَالَ: كَانَ رَسُوْلُ اللهِ ﷺ لَا يُحَدِّثُ حَدِيثًا إِلَّا تَبَسَّمَ.

رَوَاهُ الْإِمَامُ أَحْمَدُ.

Abū al-Dardā' ﵁ said: **"The Messenger of Allah ﷺ would always smile when speaking."**

Narrated by Imam Aḥmad.[100]

وَرَوَى الطَّبَرَانِيُّ عَنْ جَابِرِ بْنِ سَمُرَةَ ﵁، قَالَ: كَانَ رَسُولُ اللهِ ﷺ لَا يَنْبَعِثُ فِي الضَّحِكِ.

Ṭabarānī reports that Jābir ibn Samurah ﵁ said: **"The Messenger of Allah ﷺ never laughed excessively."**

**Commentary:** One of the Companions said: "The Prophet's ﷺ laugh was nothing but a smile."[101] He would never burst out laughing or guffaw. In fact, most of the time, he would just smile—but on rare occasions, he is reported to have chuckled briefly.

100 Aḥmad, 21732.
101 Tirmidhī, 3645.

Abū Bakr al-Bayhaqī writes: "He had a [lovely] gap between his two front teeth, and if his teeth showed when he laughed, they sparkled and shone like lightning."[102]

## *Twenty-Four*

عَنِ ابْنِ عَبَّاسٍ ﵄ قَالَ: كَانَ لَا يُدْفَعُ عَنْهُ النَّاسُ وَلَا يُضْرَبُوا عَنْهُ.

[ʿAbd-Allāh] ibn ʿAbbās ﵄ said: **"People would not be driven away from him (i.e., the Messenger of Allah ﷺ) nor would they be prevented from meeting him."**[103]

**Commentary**: The Prophet ﷺ was not a leader who was aloof and removed from his people. He was not inaccessible or had layers of courtiers and protocols before an ordinary man could reach him. Instead, he was a Prophet ﷺ ﴾*from amongst them*﴿ (*al-Baqarah*, 2:129) who lived with them and taught them; he sat with them, ate with them, and they shared their worries and their woes and sought his help in every matter.

---

102 Bayhaqī, *Dalāʾil al-Nubuwwah,* 1:303; *al-Shamāʾil al-Muḥammadiyyah*, 14: the wording used is "when he would speak, something like a light would emit from between his teeth."

103 *Al-Muʿjam al-Kabīr*, 10628.

Al-Munāwī writes: "This was due to his immense humility and lack of arrogance, contrary to how worldly kings treat their subjects."[104] Worldly kings who obsess over the mundane do not intermingle with their subjects and only meet them at specific times and in exceptional circumstances—whilst the Prophet ﷺ lived amongst them and thus ruled their hearts.

His humility was such that he would greet young children first. On one occasion, when a person was awestruck by the Prophet ﷺ, he comforted him by saying: "Relax. I am not a [worldly] king. I am the son of a woman who would eat dried meat."[105]

This was to make the person feel at ease, to remind them that he was not like other rulers who would make a point to show their power and strike fear in people's hearts. Instead, he was a king, unlike other kings—unique, extraordinary and peerless.

---

104 *Fayḍ al-Qadīr*, (5:234) 6888.
105 Ibn Mājah, 3312.

## Twenty-Five

عَنْ أَنَسٍ رضي الله عنه قَالَ: كَانَ رَسُوْلُ اللهِ ﷺ لَا يُسْأَلُ شَيْئًا إِلَّا أَعْطَاهُ أَوْ سَكَتَ.

رَوَاهُ الْحَاكِمُ.

Anas [ibn Mālik] رضي الله عنه said: **"If someone asked the Messenger of Allah ﷺ for anything, he would either give to them [if he had it] or else he would remain silent."**

Narrated by al-Ḥākim.[106]

رَوَى الْإِمَامُ أَحْمَدُ عَنْ أَبِي أُسَيْدٍ السَّاعِدِيِّ رضي الله عنه، قَالَ: كَانَ رَسُولُ اللهِ ﷺ لَا يَمْنَعُ شَيْئًا يُسْأَلُهُ.

Abū Usayd al-Sāʿidī رضي الله عنه said: **"The Messenger of Allah ﷺ would not refuse to grant something he was asked for."**[107]

106 *Al-Mustadrak*, 2591.
107 Aḥmad, 16056.

رَوَى الطَّبَرَانِيُّ عَنْ طَلْحَةَ ؓ، قَالَ: كَانَ رَسُوْلُ اللهِ ﷺ لَا يَكَادُ يُسْأَلُ شَيْئًا إِلَّا فَعَلَهُ.

Ṭalḥah ؓ said: **"The Messenger of Allah ﷺ was hardly asked for something except that he gave it."**[108]

**Commentary:** The Prophet ﷺ was so generous that he neither turned away the pious nor the sinful. With open arms and an open heart, he greeted all, for he held the keys to Allah's blessings in his hands. If he did not have anything to give at that particular moment, he would stay silent, and the person asking would understand that the Prophet ﷺ did not have anything at hand to give.

*He never said "no" except*
*When saying, "There is no God but Him"*
*Were it not for this*
*Then even his "no" would have been "yes".*[109]

He did not like to keep any wealth in his possession; he would seek out ways to give away gold or silver if he had any. Once, he told his companion Abū Dharr as they were passing by Mount Uḥud: "If I had gold the size of Mount Uḥud, it would not please me until not a single gold coin remained after three

108 *Al-Muʿjam al-Kabīr*, 212.
109 Farazdaq, *Dīwān al-Farazdaq*.

days—for I would distribute everything among the slaves of Allah [i.e., Muslims] except that which I would retain to pay off my debts."[110]

This does not mean that Muslims should not seek wealth absolutely. Instead, wealth should be sought to fulfil one's own needs and the needs of others. Wealth for the sake of worldly grandeur and luxury is deplorable. However, if the intention is to use it for noble causes, it is not blameworthy because actions depend upon intentions. In fact, even some of the companions of the Prophet ﷺ were extremely affluent—but they were also extremely generous with their wealth. As a scholar has said: "Wealth should be in one's hand, not in one's heart."

Al-Munāwī writes: "He would give even if he were asked for a lot. He gave in the manner of a person who did not fear poverty. Ibn al-Qayyim said: 'He was far happier when he was giving than when he was receiving.'"[111]

See comments on hadith eighteen.

110 Bukhārī, 6444.
111 *Fayḍ al-Qadīr*, (5:242) 6917.

## Twenty-Six

عَنْ سَهْلِ بْنِ حُنَيْفٍ ﵁، قَالَ: كَانَ رَسُوْلُ اللهِ ﷺ يَأْتِي ضُعَفَاءَ الْمُسْلِمِينَ يَزُورُهُمْ وَيَعُودُ مَرْضَاهُمْ وَيَشْهَدُ جَنَائِزَهُمْ.

رَوَاهُ أَبُو يَعْلَى وَالطَّبَرَانِيُّ وَالْحَاكِمُ.

Sahl ibn Ḥunayf ﵁ said: **"The Messenger of Allah ﷺ would visit destitute Muslims. He would check up on their sick and attend their funerals."**

Narrated by Abū Yaʿlā, al-Ṭabarānī, and al-Ḥākim.[112]

**Commentary:** The Prophet ﷺ was the champion of the poor. He loved and cared for the needy and the downtrodden. It is mentioned that he would go to visit the sick in the furthest parts of the city, sometimes even travelling barefoot.[113]

*The friendless and helpless, whom none care for—*
*You were made the friend and support for them!*[114]

In fact, this concern even extended to those non-believers who were receptive to the message of Islam. There was a young

112 *Al-Muʿjam al-Kabīr*, 5586; *al-Mustadrak*, 3735. I could not find this narration in the *Musnad* of Abū Yaʿlā.

113 Muslim, 925.

114 Ḥasan Riḍā, *Dhawq i Naʿat*.

Jewish boy who would serve the Prophet Muhammad ﷺ. He fell ill so the Prophet Muhammad ﷺ visited him, sat near his head, and told him to accept Islam. The young boy looked towards his father, who instructed him thus: "Listen to Abū al-Qāsim (i.e., the Prophet Muhammad ﷺ), and so the boy accepted Islam."[115]

Many forget the downtrodden and the needy, but that does not mean they are unworthy of attention and support. Kindness and assistance to those in need is an exemplary character trait that is praiseworthy in Islam.

## *Twenty-Seven*

**عَنْ عَائِشَةَ رضي الله عنها قَالَتْ: كَانَ رَسُوْلُ اللهِ ﷺ لَا يُؤْتَى بِالصِّبْيَانِ فَيُبَرِّكُ عَلَيْهِمْ وَيُحَنِّكُهُمْ وَيَدْعُو لَهُمْ.**

رَوَاهُ الْبُخَارِيُّ وَمُسْلِمٌ وَأَبُو دَاوُدَ.

Lady ʿĀ'ishah رضي الله عنها said: **"Babies would be brought to the Messenger of Allah ﷺ and he would ask for them to be blessed, perform taḥnīk on them, and pray for them."**

115 Bukhārī, 1356.

Narrated by al-Bukhārī, Muslim and Abū Dāwūd.[116]

**Commentary:** "*Taḥnīk* is to chew a date, raisin, or something similar and then rub it on the palate of the newborn child. The mouth will be kept open until some part of it reaches the oral cavity."[117]

Having a child is a joyous occasion for the parents and so the Prophet ﷺ would partake in their celebration by blessing them, performing *taḥnīk* from his own blessed mouth for the child, and praying for them. What greater gift can a person receive than this?

## *Twenty-Eight*

عَنِ ابْنِ عَبَّاسٍ رضي الله عنهما قَالَ: كَانَ رَسُوْلُ اللهِ ﷺ يَتَفَاءَلُ وَلَا يَتَطَيَّرُ وَيُحِبُّ الِاسْمَ الْحَسَنَ.

رَوَاهُ الْإِمَامُ أَحْمَدُ.

ʿAbd-Allah ibn ʿAbbās رضي الله عنهما said: **"The Messenger of Allah ﷺ would be optimistic, was not superstitious, and loved pleasant names."**

---

116 Bukhārī, 6355; Muslim, 2147; Abū Dāwūd, 5106.
117 Ibn Raslān, *Sharḥ Sunan Abī Dāwūd*, (19:362) 5106.

Narrated by Imam Aḥmad.[118]

**Commentary:** Superstition was rife among Arabs before Islam, such as: the belief that killing a snake would incite its partner to seek revenge; engaging in ornithomancy (seeking omens by observing the behaviour of birds); gouging a camel's eye out to protect the others from the evil eye; tying a string on a tree before departing on a journey—if untied upon arrival, it would mean that their spouse had been unfaithful; wearing their clothes inside out if lost on a journey believing this would help them find their path, and many more such practices.

One of the core beliefs of Islam is that everything happens according to Allah's Will. Omens and auguries will not change destiny. People lose their peace of mind looking for signs and worry and fret needlessly due to belief in bad omens (which have no basis in reality).

The Prophet ﷺ forbade Muslims from considering omens: "There is no evil omen."[119] However, he would take good signs as auspicious and this is because such signs give hope.

Al-Munāwī writes: "The Messenger of Allah ﷺ was always positive and hopeful. When he heard something good, he would take it as an auspicious sign [this was as a marker of

118 Aḥmad, 2766.
119 Bukhārī, 5422.

hope] — but he was not superstitious like the Arabs in the pagan times, who dreaded evil omens.

This is because when one is optimistic, a good sign is hope in the Mercy and Bounty of the Almighty, even if one is mistaken in their optimism; and belief in bad omens is having lost hope in the Lord Almighty and expecting something bad to befall. He loved good names not out of superstition but due to his dislike of bad names—rather than fearing the 'effect' of the bad name."[120]

A believer is never despondent. Even if he passes through a challenging phase and trying times, he will not lose hope. He will believe in Allah's Promise: ﴾*Indeed, with hardship, comes ease*﴿ (*al-Inshirāḥ*, 94:5). This inspires the believer to be patient and positive in hard times, and he is content with whatever Allah has decreed for him.

Many of us may have lived in times when life seemed bleak, matters hopeless, and there was seemingly no light at the end of the tunnel. Yet soon after, Allah removed the hardship and gave us comfort and ease. We were then happier than ever before. Thus, we realise that trials and tribulations bring with them lessons—they make us stronger and wiser. It is important to treasure these moments. When faced with adversity once more, it is vital to remember that ease will follow, just as the

---

120 *Fayḍ al-Qadīr*, (5:258) 6975.

night gives way to day. A true believer is always hopeful and optimistic.

*Do not despair! Despair is the death of knowledge and gnosis—*
*The hope of the true believer contains the divine secret of success.*[121]

## *Twenty-Nine*

عَنِ ابْنِ عَبَّاسٍ رضي الله عنهما قَالَ: كَانَ رَسُوْلُ اللهِ ﷺ يَجْلِسُ عَلَى الْأَرْضِ، وَيَأْكُلُ عَلَى الْأَرْضِ، وَيَعْتَقِلُ الشَّاةَ، وَيُجِيبُ دَعْوَةَ الْمَمْلُوكِ عَلَى خُبْزِ الشَّعِيرِ.

رَوَاهُ الطَّبَرَانِيُّ.

ʿAbd-Allāh ibn ʿAbbās رضي الله عنهما said: **"The Messenger of Allah ﷺ would sit on the floor, eat on the floor, tether his sheep, and accept the invitation of slaves in which they would present [simple food such as] barley bread."**

Narrated by al-Ṭabarānī.[122]

121 Iqbāl, *Bāl i Jibrīl.*
122 *Al-Muʿjam al-Kabīr*, 12494.

**Commentary:** The Prophet ﷺ commanded the unwavering devotion and allegiance of his companions, who were willing to make the ultimate sacrifice of their wealth, property and even their very lives at the mere gesture of his command.

Despite this, he ﷺ refused to live in a pompous manner. In fact, he even directed his companions not to stand [in respect] when he entered the room.[123] He would accept the invitation of those who were from the weakest and most destitute of society. This was to show that nobody holds superiority over another in Allah's Court except by virtue of being greater in piety and good deeds.

The fact that he did not care for a person's riches or what they had to offer him is just one facet of his immense sincerity and evidence of the truthfulness of Islam. The Prophet ﷺ was a true leader who guided towards righteousness rather than seeking power and wealth for himself. In all respects, he sought to benefit and guide the people to the truth, beauty and prosperity. He looked to see how he could give rather than how he could take.

---

123 Tirmidhī, 2754.

## Thirty

عَنْ عَائِشَةَ رضي الله عنها قَالَتْ: كَانَ رَسُوْلُ اللهِ ﷺ يَخِيطُ ثَوْبَهُ، وَيَخْصِفُ نَعْلَهُ، وَيَعْمَلُ مَا يَعْمَلُ الرِّجَالُ فِي بُيُوتِهِمْ.

رَوَاهُ الْإِمَامُ أَحْمَدُ.

Lady ʿĀ'ishah رضي الله عنها said: **"The Messenger of Allah ﷺ would patch his own garments, mend his own sandals, and would do [chores] in the house just as other men did in their homes."**

Narrated by Imam Aḥmad.[124]

**Commentary:** The Prophet ﷺ said: "A man is the guardian of his family and is responsible for his subjects; a woman is the guardian of her husband's home and his children and is responsible for them."[125]

Despite this, the Prophet ﷺ would still choose to do his own chores as much as possible, demonstrating his self-reliance and reluctance to burden others. He would not ask others to do something for him but rather do it himself.

This may not always be possible for men, especially in societies in which a man is expected to work long hours to

---

124 Aḥmad, 25341.
125 Bukhārī, 7138.

provide for his family. In these situations, he should still show appreciation to his wife for fulfilling her duties, and the wife, too, should be grateful to her husband for providing.

Even though modernist and feminist views clash with the idea of a woman as a homemaker, like drinking salt water, this brash and senseless quest for a notional 'freedom' has led to the destruction of the family structure in the West.

## *Thirty-One*

عَنْ أَنَسٍ ﷺ قَالَ: كَانَ رَسُوْلُ اللهِ ﷺ يُدْعَى إِلَى خُبْزِ الشَّعِيرِ وَالْإِهَالَةِ السَّنْخَةِ.

Anas [ibn Mālik] ﷺ said: **"The Messenger of Allah ﷺ would be invited to a meal of barley bread and stale oil [and would accept the invitation]."**[126]

**Commentary:** Can you imagine the leader of a nation today accepting the invitation of slaves and the poor? Let alone an invitation to a meal in which only simple bread is served along with stale oil. Despite being the supreme leader, our Prophet ﷺ accepted such invitations readily. On these occasions, he

126 *Al-Shamā'il al-Muḥammadiyyah*, 333.

would not utter a single word of discontent. Instead, he would honour his guests with his affable presence.

What people would give to live a life of luxury! People have committed unimaginable crimes in the pursuit of power and wealth. Yet, our Prophet ﷺ shunned such power and wealth.

It was this nature of his which prompted Edward Gibbon, the author of *The History of the Decline and Fall of the Roman Empire*, to write: "The good sense of Mahomet [Muhammad] despised the pomp of royalty: the apostle of God submitted to the menial offices of the family: he kindled the fire, swept the floor, milked the ewes, and mended with his own hands his shoes and his woollen garment. [...] On solemn occasions he feasted his companions with rustic and hospitable plenty; but in his domestic life, many weeks would elapse without a fire being kindled on the hearth of the prophet. [...] His hunger was appeased with a sparing allowance of barley-bread: he delighted in the taste of milk and honey; but his ordinary food consisted of dates and water."[127]

*The world is his dominion, yet his diet is barley bread*
*Upon the contentment of that stomach—a million salutations.*[128]

127 Gibbon, *History of the Saracen Empire*, p. 44.
128 Riḍā, *Ḥadāiq-i Bakhshish.*

## Thirty-Two

عَنْ أَبِي أَيُّوبَ الْأَنْصَارِيِّ ﵁ قَالَ: كَانَ رَسُوْلُ اللهِ ﷺ يَرْكَبُ الْحِمَارَ، وَيَخْصِفُ النَّعْلَ، وَيَرْقَعُ الْقَمِيصَ، وَيَلْبَسُ الصُّوفَ، وَيَقُولُ: مَنْ رَغِبَ عَنْ سُنَّتِي فَلَيْسَ مِنِّي.

رَوَاهُ ابْنُ عَسَاكِرَ.

Abū Ayyūb al-Anṣārī ﵁ said: **"The Messenger of Allah ﷺ would ride camels, fix his sandals, patch his own shirt, and wear wool. He would say, 'Whoever abandons my Sunnah is not from me.'"**

Narrated by Ibn ʿAsākir.[129]

**Commentary:** The Messenger of Allah ﷺ had no such want or need for anything in the world. In fact, the Messenger of Allah ﷺ actively chose to forego any worldly rule. It is mentioned that: "An Angel said: 'O Muhammad ﷺ, your Lord has sent me to you with the offer to either make you a Prophet-King or a Servant-Messenger.' The Prophet ﷺ said: 'Rather, I will be a Servant-Messenger.'"[130] On another occasion, he said: "My Lord presented the valleys of Makkah, that He would

129 *Tārīkh Madīnah al-Dimashq*, 4:77.
130 Aḥmad, 7160.

turn them into gold for me. But I said: 'No, my Lord. Rather, I will eat one day and fast the other.'"[131]

*The lofty mountains tried to tempt him by turning into gold*
*But he showed them what true loftiness is.*[132]

When a person humbles themself in front of Allah, the entire world will humble themselves for them. The Prophet ﷺ was the most humble of all, and so Allah elevated him above all of creation. The Byzantine emperor Heraclius said: "If I were sure I could reach him then, I would go to him immediately. And if I were with him then I would certainly wash his feet."[133]

Reginald Bosworth Smith, author and graduate of Oxford University, writes: "Without a standing army, without a bodyguard, without a palace, without a fixed revenue, if ever any man had the right to say that he ruled by a right Divine, it was Mohammed; for he had all the power without its instruments and without its supports."[134]

131 Tirmidhī, 2347.
132 Buṣīrī.
133 Bukhārī, 7.
134 Smith, *Mohammed and Mohammedanism*, p. 235.

## Thirty-Three

عَنْ أَنَسٍ ﵁ قَالَ: كَانَ رَسُوْلُ اللهِ ﷺ يَزُورُ الْأَنْصَارَ وَيُسَلِّمُ عَلَى صِبْيَانِهِمْ وَيَمْسَحُ رُؤُوسَهُمْ.

رَوَاهُ النَّسَائِيُّ.

Anas [ibn Mālik] ﵁ said: **"The Messenger of Allah ﷺ would visit the Anṣār, greet their children, and pat them on their heads."**

Narrated by al-Nasā'ī.[135]

**Commentary:** The Muslims who migrated from Mecca to Medina were the Muhājirūn (Emigrants), and the residents of Medina were the *Anṣār* (Helpers).

The Prophet ﷺ loved the *Anṣār* dearly; he once said: "None loves the Anṣār but a believer and none but a hypocrite hates them. Allah loves those who love them, and He hates those who hate them."[136] This was because he appreciated their sacrifices and the help they extended to the Emigrants; he let it be known that he held them dear to his heart.

135 *Al-Sunan al-Kubrā*, 8291.
136 Bukhārī, 3783.

He ﷺ would show their children kindness by engaging in a lighthearted conversation with them. He would play with them and make them laugh.

There was a toddler named Abū 'Umayr, who was the narrator's younger brother. He had a small pet bird (Nughayr) which he would play with. The Prophet ﷺ would visit them and, on such visits, play with the child and make him laugh. One day, when the Prophet ﷺ visited the house, the bird had died, and the child was sad. The Prophet ﷺ stroked the child's head and tried to lift his dampened spirit by talking to him kindly and making him laugh. He said: "O Abū 'Umayr—where is Nughayr?" The Prophet's ﷺ reassuring presence, the warmth of his words and the endearing rhyme cheered up the child and he began to laugh.

This was the mercy and gentleness of he who was mercy personified. A manifestation of Allah's Grace for the world to see.

## Thirty-Four

عَنْ عَمْرِو بْنِ الْعَاصِ ﵁ قَالَ: كَانَ رَسُوْلُ اللهِ ﷺ يُقْبِلُ بِوَجْهِهِ وَحَدِيثِهِ عَلَى شَرِّ الْقَوْمِ يَتَأَلَّفُهُ بِذَلِكَ.

رَوَاهُ الطَّبَرَانِيُّ.

ʿAmr ibn al-ʿĀṣ ﵁ said: **"The Messenger of Allah ﷺ would turn towards the worst man in the community and would speak to him [gently] in order to attract him [towards Islam and goodness.]"**

Narrated by al-Ṭabarānī.[137]

**Commentary:** Al-Munāwī explains: "He ﷺ would make them feel comfortable by giving them attention and by being gentle to them, to make them more inclined towards Islam."[138]

His care and mercy was not just for the righteous; instead, it extended to everyone—even the worst of sinners, as he has himself said: "My intercession is for the major sinners from my nation."[139]

137 Haythamī, *Majmaʿ al-Zawā'id,* 9:15, who references it to Ṭabarānī; *al-Shamā'il al-Muḥammadiyyah,* 338.

138 Bukhārī, 3783.

139 Tirmidhī, 2435.

*Lo! Here he comes, smiling towards us sinners —*
*Letting lightning burn away the crops of our misdeeds.*[140]

He was sent as a mercy to the universe; with the promise of unending hope and forgiveness—he would not turn sinners away. He would embrace them and this kindness transformed them into the most righteous of men.

We are not perfect, and we should be mindful of this when dealing with others—we all sin in some way yet we judge when others sin in a different way. Rather, we should try to rectify ourselves and the behaviour of others without being judgemental. This is because advising a fellow believer is also considered a reward in and of itself.

It is not the Prophetic way to abandon those who are indulged in sin for often times, they are those who are most in need of our help and encouragement.

140 *Ḥadāiq-i-Bakhshish.*

## Thirty-Five

عَنْ أَنَسٍ ﵁ قَالَ: كَانَ رَسُوْلُ اللهِ ﷺ يَقُوْلُ لِأَحَدِهِمْ عِنْدَ الْمُعَاتَبَةِ:
مَا لَهُ تَرِبَ جَبِيْنُهُ.

رَوَاهُ الْإِمَامُ أَحْمَدُ وَالْبُخَارِيُّ.

Anas [ibn Mālik] ﵁ said: **"When the Messenger of Allah ﷺ would reprimand someone, he would say: 'What is the matter with him? May dust cover his forehead!'"**

Narrated by Imam Aḥmad and al-Bukhārī.[141]

**Commentary:** Al-Nabahānī comments: "'May dust cover his forehead' was a commonly used Arabic proverb [to express disappointment]. It was not a curse or a prayer against someone." These were the 'most critical' words that the Prophet Muhammad ﷺ used to reprimand his Companions.

The Prophet ﷺ understood that being overly strict with people may have an adverse effect on the process of rectifying their behaviour. As sentient beings, human emotions play a significant role in our interactions with people. Recognising this truth is crucial when navigating relationships with one

141 Aḥmad, 12274; Bukhārī, 6031.

another. It is for this reason that the Prophet ﷺ was renowned for his ability to maintain a composed demeanor—a testament to this his remarkable emotional fortitude.

There are many occasions reported where Bedouins—unaware of the propriety that accompanies civic society and its norms—would speak to the Prophet Muhammad ﷺ rudely. This affront to the respect due to the Prophet ﷺ would anger his ardent Companions, so much so that they would be ready to kill the impudent foreigner. Yet, the Prophet Muhammad ﷺ would calm their fervour, teaching them forbearance through his practical example. He would engage with the Bedouin and try to make it such that all parties were pleased. It was this compassion, in an era where compassion was scarce, that changed the face of the world forever.

Many of us today know someone of exemplary character who was overcome with anger despite their best attempts to manage their composure. However, when the Prophet ﷺ was angry—and that too only for the sake of Allah—the most that he would say is: "May dust cover his forehead." Even his anger contains a lesson on the highest degrees of mercy.

## *Thirty-Six*

عَنْ ابْنِ أَبِي أَوْفَى ﷺ قَالَ: كَانَ رَسُوْلُ اللهِ ﷺ يُكْثِرُ الذِّكْرَ وَيُقِلُّ اللَّغْوَ، وَيُطِيلُ الصَّلَاةَ وَيُقْصِرُ الْخُطْبَةَ، وَكَانَ لَا يَأْنَفُ وَلَا يَتَكَبَّرُ أَنْ يَمْشِيَ مَعَ الْأَرْمَلَةِ وَالْمِسْكِينِ وَالْعَبْدِ حَتَّى يَقْضِيَ لَهُ حَاجَتَهُ.

رَوَاهُ النَّسَائِيُّ وَالْحَاكِمُ، وَرَوَاهُ الْحَاكِمُ عَنْ أَبِي سَعِيدٍ الْخُدْرِيِّ.

[ʿAbd-Allāh] Ibn Abī Awfā ﷺ said: **"The Messenger of Allah ﷺ would constantly be engaged in the remembrance of Allah and never engaged in idle talk. His prayer was lengthy and his sermons were short. He did not consider it below his stature to walk with a widow, a poor man or a slave. He would go with them and fulfil their needs."**

Narrated by al-Nasāʾī; and al-Ḥākim who narrated it from Abū Saʿīd al-Khudrī.[142]

**Commentary:** Idle talk refers to speech that is useless and futile. This does not mean all worldly matters are idle talk, and one should only speak about religious matters. One is allowed to talk about productive matters that have any benefit in this

142 *Al-Sunan al-Kubrā*, 1414; *al-Mustadrak*, 4226.

world or in the hereafter. The Prophet ﷺ would speak with his companions on a variety of matters. He would ask them about their worldly affairs and give them counsel. His speech would make them happy.

Zayd ibn Thābit, the neighbour of the Prophet ﷺ, said regarding him: "When we would speak about worldly matters, he would speak about it with us; when we would mention the Hereafter, he would speak about the Hereafter. And if we were to speak about food, he would speak about it with us as well!"[143] In another narration, it is mentioned: "He would laugh at what the Companions would laugh at and would express interest in what they were interested in."[144]

When he ﷺ would speak on these matters, it would not be vain speech, but instead he would provide his insight, for he was the wisest and most knowledgeable of all. Engaging with the Companions in this way and being interested in what they spoke about was his way of expressing his love for them—when a person loves another, they love to hear them speak. The Companions reciprocated this too, for when he ﷺ spoke, it would be as if birds were perched on their heads due to their stillness and pin-drop silence.[145]

We understand from this that it is a Sunnah to show genuine interest in people, to engage with them on topics they are

---

143 *Al-Shamāʾil al-Muḥammadiyyah*, 337.
144 *Al-Shamāʾil al-Muḥammadiyyah*, 345.
145 Abū Dāwūd, 3855.

enthusiastic about, and to partake in their joy—whilst abstaining from speech that is not permissible, such as backbiting, slander etc. If people were to act upon this, we would see our society become less self-centred and conceited and move towards becoming more empathetic, considerate, and thoughtful of others.

### *Thirty-Seven*

**عَنْ عَائِشَةَ ﵂ قَالَتْ: كَانَ رَسُوْلُ اللهِ ﷺ يَقْبَلُ الْهَدِيَّةَ وَيُثِيبُ عَلَيْهَا.**

رَوَاهُ الْإِمَامُ أَحْمَدُ وَالْبُخَارِيُّ وَأَبُو دَاوُدَ وَالتِّرْمِذِيُّ.

Lady ʿĀ'ishah ﵂ said: **"The Messenger of Allah ﷺ would accept gifts and would give gifts in return."**

Narrated by Imam Aḥmad, al-Bukhārī, Abū Dāwūd, and al-Tirmidhī.[146]

---

146 Aḥmad, 24591; Bukhārī, 2585; Abū Dāwūd, 4512; Tirmidhī, 1953.

وَرَوَى الْإِمَامُ أَحْمَدُ وَالطَّبَرَانِيُّ عَنْ عَائِشَةَ وَأَبِي هُرَيْرَةَ: إِنَّهُ كَانَ يَأْكُلُ الْهَدِيَّةَ وَلَا يَأْكُلُ الصَّدَقَةَ.

Imam Aḥmad and al-Ṭabarānī report from ʿĀʾishah and Abū Hurayrah that: **"He [the Messenger of Allah ﷺ] would eat something that was gifted, but he would not partake from that which was given as charity."**[147]

**Commentary:** Accepting gifts was a sign of Prophetic hospitality and an example of his impeccable character, which softened people's hearts towards him. He ﷺ has said elsewhere that: "Exchange gifts with each other to increase love between one another."'[148] He would not differentiate between expensive and inexpensive gifts—he would accept a draught of milk[149] or the leg of a rabbit.[150]

He ﷺ did not care about what was being gifted as much as the person gifting and the sentiment of the gift. For far greater than the gift's material value is the love borne of it. And who offered more love to his people than the Prophet ﷺ? And who loved giving more than the Prophet ﷺ?

---

147 *Al-Muʿjam al-Kabīr*, 6065; Aḥmad, 8714.
148 *Al-Adab al-Mufrad*, 94.
149 Muslim, 1123.
150 Bukhārī, 2572.

It was only befitting of his generous nature to give a gift upon receiving one. Al-Khaṭṭābī writes: "It is mentioned in the Divine Books revealed prior that the Final Prophet would accept gifts and not eat from charity. [...] And he would reciprocate gifts received so that he would not be beholden to anyone nor have someone's favour over him."[151] This is because if the Prophet ﷺ accepted gifts without reciprocating, then people might have perceived it as a reward or wage of some sort, whilst his true reward was only with Allah.

## *Thirty-Eight*

عَنْ عَائِشَةَ رضي الله عنها قَالَتْ: كَانَ رَسُوْلُ اللهِ ﷺ إِذَا بَلَغَهُ عَنْ الرَّجُلِ الشَّيْءُ لَمْ يَقُلْ: مَا بَالُ فُلَانٍ يَقُولُ؟ وَلَكِنْ يَقُولُ: مَا بَالُ أَقْوَامٍ يَقُولُونَ كَذَا وَكَذَا.

رَوَاهُ أَبُو دَاوُدَ.

Lady ʿĀ'ishah رضي الله عنها said: **"When it would reach the Messenger of Allah ﷺ that someone said something, he would not say, 'What is the matter with so-and-so that he is saying this?' Instead, he would say,**

151 Khaṭṭābī, *Maʿālim al-Sunan*, 3:168-169.

**'What is the matter with some people that they say such-and-such?'"**

Narrated by Abū Dāwūd.[152]

**Commentary:** Criticising people by name, especially in public settings, leads to them feeling personally slighted and attacked. If the aim is to rectify someone's behaviour, singling them out would have the opposite effect.

Instead, the Prophet ﷺ would make a generic statement so that the person in question would not feel that they were being targeted personally. In this way, the Prophet ﷺ would correct them without causing the person to lose face.

The Prophet ﷺ would correct people—after all, he was sent as a teacher to mankind. He would often exhort people to repent and would say it in general words: "Every son of Adam makes mistakes, and the best of them are those who repent"[153]

Ibn Raslān writes in light of this: "This was an example of good societal conduct that he ﷺ would not specifically criticise someone on a matter that displeased him, nor would he call them out by name due to his immense modesty."[154]

---

152 Abū Dāwūd, 4788.
153 Tirmidhī, 2499.
154 *Sharḥ Sunan Abī Dāwūd*, (18:445) 4788.

## *Thirty-Nine*

عَنِ ابْنِ بَكْرَةَ ﷺ قَالَ: كَانَ رَسُوْلُ اللهِ ﷺ إِذَا جَاءَ مَا يَسُرُّهُ خَرَّ سَاجِدًا شَاكِرًا لَهُ تَعَالَى.

Ibn Bakrah said: **"If the Messenger of Allah ﷺ received good news, he would go down in prostration, to thank Allah, the Exalted."**[155]

**Commentary:** When we receive a blessing or good news, we must bow down our heads in gratitude to Allah, who has bestowed these bounties upon us. Some are reminded of Allah only in difficulties and are heedless in good times. A believer remembers Allah in good times and bad times.

## *Forty*

عَنْ عَائِشَةَ ﷺ قَالَتْ: كَانَ رَسُوْلُ اللهِ ﷺ إِذَا رَأَى مَا يُحِبُّ قَالَ: الْحَمْدُ لِلهِ الَّذِي بِنِعْمَتِهِ تَتِمُّ الصَّالِحَاتُ.

Lady ʿĀ'ishah said: **"If the Messenger of Allah ﷺ encountered something that he liked he would say:**

155 Abū Dāwūd, 2774; Ibn Mājah, 1394.

**'Praise be to Allah, by Whose Grace, all good things will be perfected and made wholesome.'"[156]**

**Commentary:** In life, true happiness cannot be found in material possessions and belongings; rather, ﴾*Indeed, in the remembrance of Allah do the hearts find comfort*﴿ (*al-Ḥajj*, 22:66). In remembering our Creator, we take a look at His creation. His infinite bounties and blessings ﴾*cannot be enumerated*﴿ (*Ibrāhīm*, 14:34).

Appreciation does not mean disavowal or that a Muslim must live as an ascetic. Allah says: ﴾*And seek the final abode with what Allah has given to you, and [yet] do not forget your share from this world. And do good, as Allah has done good to you*﴿ (*al-Qaṣaṣ*, 28:77). It means that contentment and meaning - which our souls crave above all else - will not be found in material possessions.

*Do not seek joy in the glamour of modernity—*
*For I have found that the believer's ascension lies in contentment.*[157]

The Prophet ﷺ would always express his gratitude and praise Allah upon seeing what pleased him. Human beings have a tendency to overlook the blessings that Allah has bestowed

156 *Tārīkh Madīnah al-Dimashq*, 3:383; *al-Mustadrak*, 1840.
157 Iqbāl, *Bang-i Darā*.

upon them—﴾*Indeed, mankind is ungrateful*﴿ (*al-Ḥajj*, 22:66). Rather than looking at all that we have and appreciating it, we compare it with what others have and complain about what we do not have. Truly, comparison is the thief of joy.

The Prophet ﷺ would spend entire nights worshipping Allah; sometimes, his feet would swell and the skin of his feet would crack. His wife once asked him: "Why do you suffer this when Allah has protected you from sin and has forgiven the sins of others for your sake." He ﷺ replied with words to soften the hardest of hearts: "Shall I not be a grateful servant [of Allah]?"[158]

*I have violated the way of him who stayed awake the nights*
*Until his feet had complained of swelling up painfully.*[159]

The greatest in the creation, most beloved to Allah and the most blessed by Allah; the one who was protected from sin —whose intercession will deliver mankind and give them salvation—would bow down in gratitude and would worship his Creator with utmost sincerity and thankfulness. Indeed, it is only appropriate that lesser beings and sinners, especially among his followers, show gratitude by praying and prostrating to their Creator for all that He has bestowed upon them.

---

158 Bukhārī, 1130.
159 Būṣīrī, *Qaṣīda al-Burda*.

*Gratitude for the blessings of Allah is itself a great blessing*
*Upon me; and it is necessary for me to thank for that too*
*How can one attain gratitude—if the Grace of Allah does not guide him*
*Even if the days (in one's life) are many and one reaches the end of his life.*

This gratitude and loyalty must be shown through actions, by following the Prophet's ﷺ example, and by moulding ourselves and reshaping the way we think in light of the Muhammadan character and lifestyle. This is what love for Allah requires—﴾*If you love Allah, then follow me, Allah will love you and forgive you your sins*﴿ (*Āl-ʿImrān*, 3:159).

Following the Prophet ﷺ leads to Allah loving a person and when Allah loves a person, He states: "When I love him, I become the ear with which he hears, the eye with which he sees, his hand with which he grasps, his foot with which he walks. If he asked me for something, I would surely grant it to him."[160]

The Poet of the East, Dr Muḥammad Iqbāl, captures this sentiment in his poetry:

*If you are loyal to Muhammad then We are yours–*

160 Bukhārī, 6502.

*What, then is the value of this Universe? The Divine Tablet and Pen are yours!*[161]

That is, the entire Universe and all that is in it cannot compare to the honour and spiritual rank that is bestowed upon the one who shows loyalty to the Prophet Muhammad ﷺ—his words, his actions and his way. 'The Divine Tablet and Pen are yours' serves as a metaphor to show the favour and grace Allah will bestow upon a person who follows the Prophet Muhammad ﷺ. He will become one of Allah's chosen ones and his wishes will be granted by Allah as mentioned in the narration.

161 Iqbāl.

## *Bibliography*

### ARABIC

al-Aṣbahānī, ʿAbd Allāh ibn Muḥammad. *Akhlāq al-nabī wa ādābuhu*. First Edition. 4 volumes. 1418/1998.

al-Aṣbahānī, Abū Nuʿaym Aḥmad ibn ʿAbd Allāh. *Ḥilyah al-awliyā' wa ṭabaqāt al-aṣfiyā'*. 10 volumes. Dār al-Fikr and Maktabah al-Khānjī, 1416/1996.

al-ʿAsqalānī, Shihāb al-Dīn Aḥmad ibn ʿAlī ibn Ḥajar. *Fatḥ al-bārī bi sharḥ ṣaḥīḥ al-bukhārī*. First Edition. 26 volumes. Dār al-Risālah al-ʿĀlamiyyah, 1434/2013.

al-Bājūrī, Ibrāhīm ibn Muhāmmad. *Al-Mawāhib al-ladunniyah ʿalā al-shamā'il al-muḥammadiyyah*. First Edition. 1422/2001.

al-Bayhaqī, Abū Bakr Aḥmad ibn al-Ḥusayn. *al-Jāmiʿ li-shuʿab al-īmān*. First Edition. 14 volumes. Maktabah al-Rushd, 1423/2003.

—*Dalā'il al-mubuwwah wa maʿrifah aḥwāl ṣāḥib al-sharīʿah*. First Edition. 7 volumes. Dār al-Kutub al-ʿIlmiyyah, 1408/1988.

al-Bukhārī, Muḥammad ibn Ismāʿīl ibn Ibrāhīm. *al-Adab al-mufrad*. al-Maṭbaʿah al-Salafiyyah, 1375/1955.

—*al-Jāmiʿ al-ṣaḥīḥ al-musnad min ḥadīth rasūl allāh* ﷺ *wa sunanihi wa ayyāmih - Ṣaḥīḥ al-Bukhārī*. First Edition. Dār Ibn Kathīr, 1423/2002.

al-Dimashqī, Abū al-Qāsim ʿAlī ibn al-Ḥasan Ibn ʿAsākir. *Tārīkh madīnah dimashq*. First Edition. 80 volumes. Dār al-Fikr, 1415/1995.

al-Haythamī, Nūr al-Dīn ʿAlī ibn Abū Bakr. *Majmaʿ al-zawāʾid wa manbaʿ al-fawāʾid*. First Edition. 12 volumes. Dār al-Kutub al-ʿIlmiyyah, 1422/2001.

al-Khaṭṭābī, Abū Sulaymān. *Maʿālim al-sunan*. First Edition. 4 volumes. al-Maṭbaʿah al-ʿIlmiyyah, 1351/1932.

al-Maʿāfirī, Abū Muḥammad ʿAbd al-Malik ibn Hishām. *al-Sīrah al-nabawiyyah*. Dār al-Kutub al-ʿArabī, 1410/1990.

al-Munāwī, Muḥammad ʿAbd al-Raʾūf. *Fayḍ al-qadīr sharḥ jāmiʿ al-ṣaghīr*. 6 volumes. Dār al-Kutub al-ʿIlmiyyah, 1422/2001.

al-Nasāʾī, Abū ʿAbd al-Raḥmān Aḥmad ibn Shuʿayb. *Kitāb Sunan al-Kubrā*. First Edition. 12 volumes. Risālah Publishers, 1421/2001.

—*Sunan al-Nasāʾī*. Second Edition. Dār al-Ḥaḍārah, 1436/2015.

al-Naysābūrī, Abū ʿAbd Allāh Muḥammad ibn ʿAbd Allāh al-Ḥākim. *al-Mustadrak ʿalā al-ṣaḥīḥayn*. Second Edition. 5 volumes. Dār al-Kutub al-ʿIlmiyyah, 1422/2002.

al-Qārī, Nūr al-Dīn Mulla ʿAlī; [and Muḥammad Khaṭīb al-Tabrīzī]. *Mirqāt al-mafātīḥ sharḥ mishkāt al-maṣābīḥ wa yalīhī: Al-Ikmāl fī asmāʾ al-rijāl*. First Edition. 11 volumes. Dār al-Kutub al-ʿIlmiyyah, 1422/2001.

al-Qazwīnī, Abū ʿAbd Allāh Muḥammad ibn Yazīd. *Sunan Ibn Mājah*. First Edition. 2 volumes. Dār Iḥyāʾ al-Kutub al-ʿArabiyyah, 1432/2011.

al-Qushayrī, Abū al-Ḥusayn Muslim ibn al-Ḥajjāj. *al-Musnad al-ṣaḥīḥ al-mukhtaṣar al-sunan bi naql al-ʿadl ʿan al-ʿadl ilā rasūl allāh ﷺ - Ṣaḥīḥ Muslim*. First Edition. 2 volumes. Dār al-Ṭaybah, 1427/2007.

al-Ramlī, Shihāb al-Dīn Aḥmad ibn Ḥusayn ibn ʿAlī ibn Raslān. *Sharḥ sunan abī dāwūd*. First Edition. Dār al-Falāḥ, 1437/2016.

al-Shaybānī, Aḥmad ibn Muḥammad ibn Ḥanbal. *Musnad al-imām aḥmad ibn ḥanbal*. First Edition. 50 volumes. Risālah Publishers, 1422/2001.

al-Sijistānī, Abū Dāwūd Sulaymān ibn al-Ashʿath. *Sunan abī dāwud*. First Edition. 6 volumes. Dār al-Risālah al-ʿĀlamiyyah, 1430/2009.

al-Ṭabarānī, Abū al-Qāsim Sulaymān ibn Aḥmad. *al-Muʿjam al-awsaṭ*. First Edition. 10 volumes. Dār al-Ḥaramayn, 1415/1995.

—*al-Muʿjam al-kabīr*. Second Edition. 25 volumes. Maktabah ibn Taymiyyah, 1404/1983.

al-Tamīmī, Aḥmad ibn ʿAlī. *Musnad abū yaʿlā al-mawṣilī*. Second Edition. 16 volumes. Dār al-Ma'mūn li al-Turāth, 1410/1989.

al-Tirmidhī, Abū ʿĪsā Muḥammad ibn ʿĪsā. *al-Jāmiʿ al-mukhtaṣar min al-sunan ʿan rasūl allāh ﷺ wa maʿrifah al-ṣaḥīḥ wa al-maʿlūl wa mā ʿalayhi al-ʿamal - Jāmiʿ al-Tirmidhī*. Second Edition. Bayt al-Afkār al-Dawliyyah, 1424/2003.

—*al-Shamā'il al-muḥammadiyyah*. Third Edition. Dār al-Ḥadīth, 1408/1988.

al-Zabīdī, al-Sayyid Muḥammad ibn Muḥammad al-Murtaḍā. *Itḥāf al-sādah al-muttaqīn bi sharḥ iḥyā' ʿulūm al-dīn*. Beirut, Lebanon: Maṭbaʿah Muṣṭafā al-Bābī al-Ḥalabī - Maṭbaʿah al-Maymūniyyah, 1311/1894.

al-Zuhrī, Muḥammad ibn Saʿd ibn Manīʿ. *Kitāb al-Ṭabaqāt al-kabīr*. First Edition. 11 volumes. Maktabah al-Khānjī, 1421/2001.

## ENGLISH

Gibbon, Edward. *History of the Saracen Empire.* Queen Square: Alex Murrray and Son, 1870.

Goethe, Johann Wolfgang von. *Notes and Essays for a Better Understanding of the West-East Divan.* State University of New York Press, 2010.

Lamartine, Alphonse de. *History of Turkey.* New York: D. Appleton & Company, 1855.

Lane Poole, Stanley. *Studies in a Mosque.* Second Edition. Eden, Remington & Company, 1893.

Carlyle, Thomas. *On Heroes, Hero-Worship, and the Heroic in History.* Yale University Press, 2013.